MOMENTS FOR
THOSE WHO HAVE
LOST A
LOVED ONE

New Life Live! Meditations

MOMENTS FOR

THOSE WHO HAVE

LOST *a*

LOVED ONE

LOIS MOWDAY RABEY

introduction by STEPHEN ARTERBURN

NAVPRESS®

BRINGING TRUTH TO LIFE

The Navigators is an international Christian organization. Our mission is to reach, disciple, and equip people to know Christ and to make Him known through successive generations. We envision multitudes of diverse people in the United States and every other nation who have a passionate love for Christ, live a lifestyle of sharing Christ's love, and multiply spiritual laborers among those without Christ.

NavPress is the publishing ministry of The Navigators. NavPress publications help believers learn biblical truth and apply what they learn to their lives and ministries. Our mission is to stimulate spiritual formation among our readers.

© 2004 by Lois Rabey

Published in association with the literary agency of Alive Communications, Inc., 7680 Goddard Street, Suite 200, Colorado Springs, Colorado, 80920.

NAVPRESS, BRINGING TRUTH TO LIFE, and the NAVPRESS logo are registered trademarks of NavPress. Absence of ® in connection with marks of NavPress or other parties does not indicate an absence of registration of those marks.

ISBN 1-57683-568-5

Cover design by David Carlson Design
Cover photo by Jules Frazier / Getty Images
Creative Team: Dan Rich, Steve Halliday, Cara Iverson, Glynese Northam

Some of the anecdotal illustrations in this book are true to life and are included with the permission of the persons involved. All other illustrations are composites of real situations, and any resemblance to people living or dead is coincidental.

Unless otherwise identified, all Scripture quotations in this publication are taken from the HOLY BIBLE: NEW INTERNATIONAL VERSION® (NIV®). Copyright © 1973, 1978, 1984 by International Bible Society. Used by permission of Zondervan Publishing House. All rights reserved. Other versions used include: the *New King James Version* (NKJV). Copyright © 1982 by Thomas Nelson, Inc. Used by permission. All rights reserved.

Rabey, Lois Mowday.
   Moments for those who have lost a loved one / Lois Mowday Rabey.
      p. cm. -- (New life live meditations)
   ISBN 1-57683-568-5
   1. Consolation. 2. Bereavement--Prayer-books and devotions--English. I. Title. II. Series.
   BV4905.3.R33 2004
   242'.4--dc22

                          2004000091

Printed in the United States of America

3 4 5 6 7 8 9 10 11 / 09 08 07 06

FOR A FREE CATALOG OF
NAVPRESS BOOKS & BIBLE STUDIES,
CALL 1-800-366-7788 (USA)
OR 1-800-839-4769 (CANADA)

CONTENTS

There are few things in life, if anything, that are more painful than the death of someone you love. It feels so final, and no amount of manipulation or prayer or pleading will change the reality of death. It is confusing because you often vacillate between anger and sadness. It is hard to identify just how you feel. Often the feeling is of abandonment. You wonder how you can make it without this person in your life. Whatever you feel, you want it to be over with quickly. You want the pain of loss to go away now. But it won't. It continues to sting, and right when you think you're beyond it, another wave of suffocating pain moves you back into despair. At its worst, you have to tell yourself to breathe; you have to tell yourself to just keep going for one more day.

People will tell you that you're not alone, but it does not matter. It feels as though you are. They tell you that God is there for you, but what you wanted was for God to prevent this great loss, and you wonder why He didn't. They even tell you that "God will bring tremendous good from it all," but you wonder why someone you love had to die for this "good" to occur. You don't care about good that is happening tomorrow when you hurt so badly that you want to die today. It seems as though everyone around you wants to come up with ultimate solutions for forgetting your grief and feeling great by morning. But there are no words that dissolve the reality of pain or make it go away. You don't need more people saying things. You just need some people to give you the time and space to feel the depths of despair and be there for you rather than make superficial attempts to fix you. There is never a quick fix for a heart broken by the death of a loved one.

My father died when he was sixty-eight. It was at a time when he and I were just beginning to forge a deeper bond man-to-man. He had begun to share his feelings about the lives we had lived. I admired him for courageously helping my brother, who died from AIDS in my parents' home. Dad was up at night with Jerry, but he never complained; he just did what a loving father had to do. He went above and beyond what most fathers would do.

He had been a good father, but he was a fantastic grandfather. He and my daughter had a very special relationship. She loved him very much, and when she set eyes on him, her mother and I were of little significance to Madeline. Her days were full of laughter and fun when her granddad was there. She loved him and needed him, and when he died, she felt it. Her way of dealing with it was to say, "Granddad held on to a bunch of balloons and flew up into the clouds to be with Jesus."

I hurt for Madeline, I hurt for Mom, and I hurt for me. There were so many things I wanted to talk to him about and do with him, but he died too soon for me to put in my requests. I did not cry at first. I did not even feel the loss at first. But when I saw my dad lying in a coffin with an American flag on top, sent from the navy, I burst into deep heaving sobs of grief. They did not stop for several weeks. At their worst, it was just me, my pain, my memories, and the belief that even though I did not feel God's presence, He was there for me.

You may be feeling some of the same things I felt. You may be wondering where God is in your loss. You may be confused about how you feel and how you will make it. If so, I hope this book will be of encouragement to you. There are not so many answers as there are reflections and directions for your consideration. Like a great friend with no preconceived ideas of how you should feel or how fast you should heal, this book is designed to just be there for you when you need it.

My prayer is that you will find some comfort within these pages. If you do, please pass it along to someone else, because the one thing we can be sure of in this world is that others will eventually walk the painful path of grief. If you need someone to talk to, please call us at 1-800-NEW-LIFE, where you'll always find someone who cares.

— STEPHEN ARTERBURN
Founder, New Life Ministries

PREFACE

He was thirty-four years old, in excellent health, and a loving husband and father. On a sunny December morning, he, two friends, and an experienced pilot took off on a hot-air-balloon ride, with wives and children waving excitedly from the ground. Within fifteen minutes, all four people in the balloon lay dead. Their airy craft of delight had turned into an inferno after hitting power lines.

The healthy thirty-four-year-old was my husband, Jack.

My daughters, Lisa and Lara, were seven and ten years old when they witnessed the death of their father. As I gathered them in my arms and promised them that we would be okay, I found myself in a situation I had never anticipated.

Jack and I had met in high school — he, a hotshot basketball star, and I, a cheerleader. I felt in awe of him, but he paid little attention to me in those glory days of athletic fame. After high school we attended nearby colleges, and romance blossomed.

We married before graduating, and I quit school and got a job so he could finish college — a typical, lovestruck scenario of the mid-1960s. Our daughters soon came along, and I felt content to be a stay-at-home mom married to the former big man on campus.

When tragedy struck, Jack owned a small insurance agency, we were active in our local church, and we enjoyed a comfortable life in Florida. The girls and I had given the balloon ride to Jack as a Christmas present. Two of Jack's friends in the insurance agency had joined him, eagerly participating in the surprise kept secret from Jack until the morning of the ride.

He had hugged me just before stepping into the balloon basket and said, "This is the perfect gift!" How could any of us have imagined that within minutes he would be gone?

Lisa and Lara both have husbands and families now, with seven children between them, and I am remarried.

I experience a full life, for which I am deeply grateful; yet, at the same time, the loose threads of grief still wisp around my soul and sting me when I least expect it. A grandchild smiles and seems the image of his Grandpa-Jack-in-heaven. A scene in a movie sets off a memory that brings tears to my eyes. One of my daughters cries because her father will never play with her children.

I am not robbed of joy, but I live where you live: in the land of those who have suffered the loss of a loved one.

I pray that these devotions will play a part in your healing. I have laced them with my story and the stories of many others who have suffered devastating loss. Along with truthfulness about pain, the stories hold great hope from those of us who have been where you are.

JESUS MAKES THE DIFFERENCE

Precious in the sight of the LORD is the death of his saints.

PSALM 116:15

I can imagine that these words from Psalm 116 stir some mixed emotions for you as you face life without your loved one. Your loss doesn't seem "precious" to you; it has left you feeling devastated. These words even seem contradictory, because the Bible calls death an enemy. Why would Scripture record this sentiment and attribute it to God?

Only one answer: Jesus conquered death. Those who trust in Him move past death to eternal life in the very presence of the Lord. Our loss is heaven's gain.

"But I want my loved one back," you say to God in honest confession.

I remember well the early days of loss. My broken heart didn't much care about being unselfish and willingly accepting the growth in heaven's population (at my expense).

And yet, as I calmed my spirit and settled my emotions, I *could* find comfort in the words of this psalm. I could picture Jack entering into the presence of the Lord and running into the arms of the One who loved him more than I did. Seeing Jack as precious in God's eyes softened the ache in my own empty arms. I wanted my pain to go away as quickly as possible, but I felt happy for the victory over death that Jack enjoyed.

The pain of loss lingers, but that reality isn't as bad as it sounds. After all, it is because of love that loss is so painful. You will eventually heal and learn to live with the scar on your soul, but you will always be touched by the memory of the presence of that missing loved one.

Pain lessens, and healing brings great comfort and freedom. You keep breathing and moving and growing, and one day, joy blooms where only sorrow lived.

None of us would choose to lose loved ones just so that they could be with God in heaven. But how unbelievable that hope lives in us in the face of death! Death pierces our lives in this fallen world, but heaven awaits us in the next.

Maybe you are reading this and you feel unsure if your loved one lives in heaven. We are not called to judge. I believe that God touches the hearts of people beyond what we can see or hear. We haven't yet moved to the other side of death, so we don't know what mysteries of God's love might be revealed there.

Faith in Christ purchases our place in heaven, but we cannot know what happens in the souls of dying people. Only God treads that mysterious land. He certainly has the power to reveal Himself to them without our knowledge. Leave your loved one in God's hands and move toward the healing He offers you.

If you don't know Jesus personally, now is the time to invite Him into your own life and trust Him as your Savior. He will walk with you through and beyond your grief. Admit to Him your own failings and accept His gift of life eternal as His beloved child.

KEEP BREATHING

Praise be to the God and Father of our Lord Jesus Christ! In his great mercy he has given us new birth into a living hope through the resurrection of Jesus Christ from the dead.

1 PETER 1:3

I sat behind the desk in Jack's office, mail sliding precariously near the edge as a mountain of envelopes filled every inch of surface space. Only four days had passed since the hot-air-balloon accident took Jack's life and the lives of his two business associates. The building custodian had been putting the mail on Jack's desk each night as he tidied up the three empty offices that had nothing to be tidied but a growing pile of mail.

I met that day with my attorney, my financial adviser, several insurance representatives, and my pastor, who gave moral support. At the end of the day, I left the office with eighteen pages of yellow legal pad notes — my to-do list related to Jack's business, all entries needing attention as soon as possible. Other to-do lists — for the house, car, children, and personal bills — waited at home.

The death of a loved one leaves an enormous void. The emotional void overwhelms us during those early days of loss, but soon the practicalities of life move in and demand attention. If you have lost a spouse, the roles that he or she used to fill now produce unending chores for you. Even if you lost someone else, your feelings of loss often impair your ability to fulfill the most routine tasks.

You may live in the midst of painful emotions that compete with practical needs. When you look at your responsibilities, you don't know where to start. "Urgent" and "more urgent" needs clamor for your attention.

Prior to Jack's death, I prided myself on my organizational skills and my ability to finish my daily to-do list. As my emotions drained my energy and my lists multiplied, however, I gave myself permission to do (or not do) things differently.

You may need to do the same thing. It really may be impossible to handle everything piled on your plate in the way you used to or in the time you slotted for it. Looking at the whole pile may overwhelm you. Take a breath, do what you can, and leave the rest for another day. You've suffered a trauma that requires making changes you likely never had anticipated, and one of those changes is to think differently about how you do things.

Allow yourself the freedom to alter your priorities and relieve pressure. You may not be able to maintain the activities you enjoyed before your loss. You may not have the time or energy to be the friend you used to be. Eventually, the pile of responsibilities will diminish and life will become more balanced.

In the meantime, relax and give God room to give you "new birth into a living hope." When you feel overwhelmed to the point of exhaustion, you may be unable even to receive the blessings God wants to give you.

"New birth" implies that you will receive a blessing that you can't even imagine. It's *new*. It's not even born in you — yet. And "living hope" breathes desire into your broken heart.

So, keep breathing — slowly, deeply — from the rich source of relationship with the living God.

New Benchmarks

I remember the days of long ago;
I meditate on all your works
and consider what your hands have done.

PSALM 143:5

Remember how slowly time passed when you were a child? A year seemed an eternity filled with many benchmarks spaced far apart. Years tended to run from the beginning of the school year until the end of the school year, with summer vacation languishing between the compulsory work of young life.

By the time we entered high school, we slipped easily into the routine of homework, the fun of fall football games, and the anticipation of the first long weekend of the school year when Thanksgiving rolled around. Soon after, the bigger break of the Christmas holidays marked winter's onset and almost half of the year gone by.

During college or early career days, circumstances determined benchmarks more than the holiday calendar did. In those years, most of us married and began our families or pursued jobs that determined how we would live out our futures.

As we look back, undoubtedly we well remember the time we

first heard about Jesus and understood the gospel. Our spiritual birthday marked a significant event that ranked right up near the top with marriage dates and the arrival of children. From a spiritual perspective, we can look back and marvel at God's direction in our lives.

And then we suffer the loss of a loved one.

All other benchmarks suddenly slide down the long list of our significant life events, and the date of loss moves to the top. Our life gets defined as "before our loss" and "after our loss." The date on the calendar when our loved one left us glares in bold print, and all other dates blur into endless days.

We now not only marvel at God's direction in our lives but we also wonder how this loss could have touched us. Our spiritual perspective seems fuzzy, even when we feel God's presence in supernatural ways.

It may seem that never again will events in life bear the weight that the loss of our loved one created. But, in time, new benchmarks will emerge. They will never obscure the date of our loss, but they will become significant and meaningful in our life after loss.

New celebrations will spring to life as years pass and healing takes place. We will again look forward to family holidays when we remember our loved one, but deep joy will replace the sting of death. We will even be able to look back and "remember the days of old" that include that day of our loss, and the pain of it will be more a memory than a piercing wound.

Time also seems to move faster. The long days of summer speed by and one Christmas seems barely over when the next one peeks around the corner. We can see another benchmark in the future: the time when we will reunite with our loved one and the last tendrils of pain will fall away. We can be in awe of the greatest of all God's works on our behalf and thank Him that all of our days this side of heaven amount to just a dot on the calendar of eternity.

LIVING IN LIMBO

My comfort in my suffering is this: Your promise preserves my life.

PSALM 119:50

I remember being a teenager at a school dance. Jack would stand on one side of the gym with the guys, while I stood in an opposite corner with all the girls. The innocence of youth accentuated the delicious desire devoid of lust but full of romance. The event of the evening: He would ask me to slow dance with him to the recorded strains of Nat King Cole crooning "Unforgettable."

He'd strut across the floor with the confident air of the assured athlete that he was. I'd hold my breath and try to appear nonchalant. Never looking directly at him, I'd make small talk with one of my girlfriends who awaited another boy of her choosing to single her out for a dance.

He wouldn't say a word as the distance between us closed to within inches, but he'd put out his hand in my direction, a silent gesture of invitation. My hand in his, we'd walk to the center of the gym floor and my anticipated moment would become reality.

And there I'd be, some fifteen years later, dancing alone in my bedroom. The music would play in my head, a pillow my only partner. The teenage feelings would bubble up from some deep reservoir of stored memories as tears spilled onto my pillow. The traces of his aftershave might linger on a pillowcase that had held his head countless times over the thirteen-plus years of our marriage.

In the limbo of loss, I would remember those moments as if he were there holding me. I had not yet moved to the place of contentment when memories no longer evoked the sense of his presence. I knew intellectually that he was gone, but I felt as if he were still with me.

Transitioning from intellectually understanding the reality of loss to actually living in the present with the reality of loss takes time. It does not occur at the moment of separation.

You undoubtedly have had such moments, too, and perhaps still do. Your longing transports you from thinking to feeling to living again — almost — with your loved one. You ache with the knowledge of loving someone and being loved. A child you bore, a sibling you fought with, a parent you idolized, a spouse you adored. Your imaginings are uniquely yours, but all those who have lost a loved one share the experience. Even though we never tell anyone about those moments of reliving the past, we go there and linger.

But we must not linger long. It is a place only to learn to let go, to say good-bye, to pull ourselves away from the feelings of the presence of our loved one. We cannot stay at this place, for it is not real. Our loved one lives elsewhere.

The bittersweet comfort we find in that limbo must give way to the comfort that God provides. His promises manifest themselves in our lives when we accept our loss and open our hearts to His healing touch.

His Word gives us hope and life. We return to the land of the living and move through our grief to wholeness. We no longer need time spent in the limbo between memory and reality, and we can now walk steadily on the solid ground of God's love.

IN THE MIDDLE OF THE NIGHT

In him was life, and that life was the light of men. The light shines in the darkness.

JOHN 1:4-5

For years after her father died, my daughter Lara slept with a light on in her bedroom. I tried to calm her fears and convince her that she didn't need the light, but to no avail. We prayed and read Bible stories and talked about guardian angels. She still wanted the light. Fear gripped her young heart and threatened the security she had felt when her father was alive.

Something about darkness conjures up feelings of fear, doubt, and dread. The setting of the sun magnifies the worries of the day-light hours. Our minds escape the limits of reason and rampage across the night skies to the worst possible conclusions.

The angel of death rides most confidently into the mind that tries to sleep in the dark. The light of Christ may fade in the absence of man-made light but lives on inside the believer. A struggle ensues that results in disturbed sleep. Imaginations spin from the truth of God's love to the possibility of more loss, and so we toss and turn.

I remember people telling me it wasn't good for Lara to sleep with the light on, that she needed to overcome her fears by learning to sleep in the dark. For a while I believed this counsel. Then I concluded that the comfort of a light seemed as much a provision from the Lord as any other temporary human comfort.

I feel the same way about adults who struggle with nighttime demons. Turn on a light! The loss of a loved one wreaks havoc on your very soul. Your body also bears the trauma of severe pain. Darkness can magnify the stress you live with each day. So if you find it helpful to sleep with a light on, do so.

We often leave nightlights on for little children so they will sleep more securely. When you have lost a loved one, your trust wavers and, like a child, you need to *learn* to feel more secure in the dark — a darkness more spiritual than physical. As God works His healing in your soul, security will return. The physical darkness so closely associated with spiritual darkness will lose its power over you.

The One who is the light of the world protects you, and awareness of that protection will fill your soul. God has defeated both death and the darkness that can breed fears and turn the middle of the night into a nightmare. The light of His presence lives in you and gives you rest, even in the darkness.

In the meantime, turn on whatever light you need to feel more peaceful. Pray and read Scripture before going to bed, but give yourself time to adjust to the fears of the dark — and know they will pass.

DO PEOPLE KNOW
WHAT THEY HAVE?

The LORD is gracious and compassionate.

PSALM 111:4

We take many of the blessings of life for granted. Before losing a loved one, we assume their presence in our lives will continue well into the distant future. Then when they are gone, an awareness of our loss consumes us. Reminders torment us: toys in the driveway, noise in the hall, the dinner table set for the whole family, the other side of the bed rumpled, the interruption of our own thoughts.

A widow once told me that women who complain of snoring husbands have never buried one. Another young woman who had suffered a miscarriage found the complaints of her pregnant friends piercing.

We all unthinkingly complain about the disturbances of our lives, but when we lose a loved one, we find ourselves yearning for such welcome disturbances. If only the silence of loss would resound once again with the voice of our loved one! If only former annoyances disrupted our daily routine!

Added to the vacuum of our lives is the awareness that others often don't seem to appreciate what they have. They act and live like we did before our loss. The precious gift of life seems so normal that its value slips beneath their consciousness.

In much the same way that we take other people for granted, we can grow complacent in our awareness of the Lord's grace and compassion. His goodness so fills our everyday lives that we don't notice its presence.

The sobering impact of loss moves that grace and compassion into sharp focus. Our vision centers on God's provision, which enables us to take one more breath. We take very little for granted and rely totally on spiritual resources to carry us through this valley. When filled with the reality of our reliance on God, we can look around us and wonder why the world keeps turning with so little apparent acknowledgment that God even exists.

If we don't take precaution, annoyance may grip us and turn to bitterness when we see the way people take God's goodness for granted. Forgetting that we tended to do the same thing before our loss, we look at friends and family with "righteous" indignation — but our indignation often carries overtones of judgmentalism that the Lord finds distasteful.

Our suffering doesn't give us the right to condemn, even silently. Better that it would lead us to compassion for people who miss the blessings of God that now seem so evident to us. If we've lost a child, we cringe at the angry words of an impatient mother to her whining toddler. If we've lost a spouse, we listen to complaints of a husband or wife and wish we could help them realize the value of companionship. If a dear friend is gone, we grieve when we see friendships dissolve over disagreements that could be resolved.

Most of the time, we hesitate to voice our feelings. Reminders of God's goodness in the midst of griping might ring of sanctimonious verse quoting.

It is, perhaps, best for us to say nothing. We can pray that our own spirits would relinquish feelings of judgment and that the spirits of others might be touched with an awareness of the grace and compassion of the Lord evident in so much of their lives. We can pray that they would not have to suffer loss to truly appreciate their loved ones.

PRECIOUS TEARS

Put my tears into Your bottle.

PSALM 56:8 (NKJV)

Tall, dense hedges border many of the narrow roads in western Ireland. Fragile, delicate fuchsia blossoms burst forth in brilliant reds and purples in the late spring and summer, covering the hedges with a profusion of shimmering colors.

The tiny flowers tremble in winds blown in from the Atlantic Ocean and endure the drenching rains so often associated with Irish weather. The fuchsia blossoms resemble tiny droplets, like tears, falling from the lush green of the hedges. Their vibrant color reminds some of drops of blood, but to me, it seemed more that the hedges wept, perhaps as much for joy as sorrow.

To look at them, you might think these delicate flowers would blow apart at the first wisp of wind. They swing and sway in the ever-changing Irish weather, almost continually buffeted by wind.

While taking a close-up photograph, I carefully plucked a blossom off a bush. To my surprise, it quite easily withstood being handled. The surprisingly sturdy fuchsia blossoms endure far more than one would imagine.

The tears we shed when we lose a loved one disappear into

tissues and handkerchiefs, absorbed away from view. They seem fragile, almost irrelevant in and of themselves, except as evidence of deep pain.

But Psalm 56:8 tells us that our tears are stored in bottles and kept in heaven. They are precious in the sight of the Lord. Like the delicate-looking fuchsia blossoms, they endure. We do not shed them in vain. Our tears serve a purpose. They water the garden of our grief and help to transform sorrow into joy. Seeds of joy rest beneath the surface due to the pain of our loss, but they remain deeply rooted in the rich soil of Christ's love.

As we weep over our loss, we release the healing power of that love into our hurting souls. Pent-up emotions break out of containment, and the power of death's grip lessens. After a good cry, we feel drained, exhausted. Like the windblown flower, we remain connected to the source of our strength despite a terrible assault.

The Lord lives in us and nothing can pull us away from Him. He gathers our tears and keeps them as evidence of our sorrow and His healing power.

A Child's Perspective

We should be called children of God.

1 JOHN 3:1

The lilting Irish melody of the hymn "Be Thou My Vision" played softly on the portable CD player on the back deck of my daughter's house. A misty rain fell on our little group, adding to the melancholy of the moment.

Justin, our oldest grandchild, was five years old at the time and had insisted that this event take place. Lisa, his mom, felt reluctant, so our close family friend Aunt Susan and I made the arrangements. Justin wanted a "party" to commemorate the burial of the remains of their family dog, Murphy.

From Justin's perspective, Murphy should be honored and given some special moments at the end of her life. He had asked each adult to bring a favorite food item of Murphy's. Aunt Susan brought M&M's, Aunt Lara brought green seedless grapes, and I brought homemade chocolate chip cookies. We wrapped these items in varying fashions and placed them in the shallow grave along with the pewter container holding Murphy's ashes. At Justin's further request, the music played and everyone said something nice about Murphy. At my husband's suggestion, Justin's parents had purchased a tree that we planted to mark Murphy's resting place. Next to the tree we placed a specially ordered stone that had her name, date of birth, and date of death written on it.

Lisa feels somewhat uncomfortable with visible displays of grief and had tried in vain to dissuade Justin from having this party. When she asked him why he wanted to do it this way, he replied, "It's what we did when Grandpa died." His paternal grandfather had died some months before, and Justin had attended the church service and "party" held at our house afterward. Some thirty members of the family had brought food, talked lovingly about Justin's grandpa, and sung traditional hymns around the piano. Laughter had filled our home as we recounted fond memories and looked forward to the day we would all reunite.

And so, on a mildly rainy Sunday afternoon in August of that same year, we commemorated the life of Murphy Miller, a beautiful, loving Akita who had blessed the family for a short five years, arriving just a few months before Justin did.

As we each shoveled a small amount of dirt into the shallow grave, filled with sweets and fruit suitable for the most discriminating canine, we cried. Lisa, too, cried and hugged Justin. It provided a healing moment filled with love for a lost pet and love and remembrance for a grandfather whose memorial service and the gathering that followed gave a child a perspective of loss that included a "party."

As the children of God, we — like chronologically young children — might do well to view life and death with the simplicity of the innocent. Justin's sadness about the loss of both his grandfather and his dog resided next to his belief that those he loved now live in heaven and that he would see them again. Of course, youth contributes greatly to simplistic thinking, but sometimes we can experience heavenly understanding more easily when we seek with the heart of a child.

I understand, too, that we expect the loss of an older grandparent and that the loss of a pet cannot be compared with the loss of a human being. But the expression of grief that Justin showed in these losses gave the adults around him a cathartic moment. Watching a child deal with loss — and imitating it, at least to a degree — cannot but invite hope into the days that follow.

NORMAL DOESN'T
ALWAYS MEAN EASY

There is a time for everything, and a season for every activity under heaven: a
time to be born and a time to die.

ECCLESIASTES 3:1-2

You now face another day since the loss of your loved one.
Undoubtedly, chores and errands fill your lists of things to do — a
wide range of activities that fall into the category of "normal." And
yet, nothing feels really normal. Every activity carries new feelings,
and even though you try to act just as you always have, you experience every moment without your loved one.

Some days you just long to feel normal again, to go about your
day feeling the familiarity of routines done over and over again for
years. Wouldn't it be nice to go to the grocery store and not wince
as you pass over that item you used to always buy? Or to leave for
work and not pause at the door for a final farewell from one who is
no longer there? *To feel normal again . . .*

But Scripture tells us that loss *is* normal. There is a time for
every purpose under heaven. Seasons move through the world of
nature, and death touches each of us.

I think we confuse normal with easy. We make assumptions

that normal life is pain free, that somehow we are entitled to a smooth road if we drive through life obediently.

In the United States, much of our culture supports these assumptions. Our high standard of living brings us countless conveniences. Advertisements tell us that we can have it all and imply that having it all secures happiness. Our culture does not acknowledge the piercing reality of the normalcy of loss.

When we lose a loved one and the normal life we expected vanishes, we feel surprised at the need to figure out how to live in a way that seems abnormal. Our surprise increases when we see that soon after the memorial service, others around us often want to avoid even mentioning our loss. Dealing with death doesn't seem normal to them, either.

When we accept death as a normal, though disruptive, part of life, God's comfort can touch each of us, sooner or later. This realization doesn't diminish the depth of pain we feel, of course, but it does remind us that we share the common ground of human experience. We weep when we see evening news reports of whole communities suffering from starvation and disease. We remember the faces of children wandering the war-torn streets of elsewhere.

Death by anything other than old age seems unfair, but it happens all the time. Our fallen world rips the life from many before they grow old. And those who do grow old eventually slip away as their human wrappings fail to sustain them.

Normal is not easy, but it is inclusive. So we become more sensitive, more caring. And we feel more appreciative when our normal

IN LOVE WITH JESUS

I love the LORD, for he heard my voice.

PSALM 116:1

Most of us can probably remember the first time we fell in love. It may have been of the "puppy" variety, but our emotions ran wild and fueled thoughts of devotion and lifelong faithfulness. The very sight of the adored one caused our heart to race and palms to sweat. Perhaps the object of our affection didn't even know about our feelings. We daydreamed and fell asleep at night with thoughts of the one with whom we felt so smitten.

You may note similar feelings welling up inside of you when you think back to the time you invited Jesus into your life. Unlike human love with all its ups and downs, loving Jesus means being loved unconditionally in return. He noticed us before we understood anything about His desire to enjoy a relationship with us. Once understood, though, the offer amazed us: communion with the living God, who brings a spiritual reality to life that can transform us, as well as the promise of eternal life when we leave this world.

When you lose a loved one, it's good to ponder the love relationship that now brings you through this dark valley, to remember days include moments of joy. We do not take good times for granted but know that in the normal course of every life, loss happens.

Our loss is unique, perhaps unexpected, untimely — but we are not alone, either humanly or spiritually.

those early days of first love and revisit the feelings of fullness you had when Jesus first came to live in your heart.

Remember how amazed you were when you encountered Jesus in a personal way, when He moved from being the object of a Sunday school lesson and instead became the Offerer of a perfect gift? He whispered to your spirit and then you looked around to see if He was speaking to someone else. *Me? Are you asking* me *to invite You into my life?*

And then He heard you, just as we read in today's verse. You prayed and your heart nearly burst when He answered your prayers. The touch of His love changed you. Your circumstances may not have changed, but you did.

Now you are hurting, but He loves you still. You probably have moments when your awareness of His presence almost transports you to heaven with your departed loved one and your gratitude for your relationship with Jesus knows no limits. At other times, Jesus may seem very distant. It may seem as if He no longer hears you. You doubt that real love could let such a loss happen. I have no answers to explain your loss. Theologians tell us that we live in a fallen world. But you probably feel that God, being God, could have chosen to do things differently. No amount of spiritual logic seems to adequately respond to the hurt in your heart.

And so when answers seem elusive and God seems far away, remember your first love. Look back at the Jesus you invited into your heart, and accept the love He still offers. It is unconditional, even if not totally comprehended. Our limited ability may muddy our understanding of God's love, but His love endures. Remember the fullness you felt when you first invited Him to rule in your heart, and turn your heart over to Him again.

NO ONE REPLACES
YOUR LOVED ONE

Suppose one of you has a hundred sheep and loses one of them. Does he not leave
the ninety-nine in the open country and go after the lost sheep until he finds it?
LUKE 15:4

We all know the saying that goes something like this: "I felt badly that I had no shoes until I saw a man who had no feet."

The saying tries to encourage gratitude for what we do have and keep us from focusing on what we don't have. Sometimes, though, I think we take this statement far from its intended meaning. We point out the goodness that remains in the life of a hurting person in an attempt to help him or her feel better about the loss.

"At least you have other children," we say to the parent who has lost a child.

"Well, you had a lot of years together," we say to the aging spouse who has lost a mate.

"Now he's out of his suffering," we say to the survivor of a person who'd suffered for a long time with some nasty illness.

These statements may all be true — but such words inflict pain instead of offering comfort. They imply that something good ought to replace the loss of a loved one.

We don't read in Scripture that the shepherd of a large flock sat back and happily counted the sheep he had when another one strayed off. That one sheep was vitally important as an individual, so the shepherd left his flock to go looking for the single lost sheep.

We can't soften the loss of a loved one by counting the number of people, even people in the same role, who remain. Realizing this truth can free us from guilt and help us to accept the depth of our loss. We can grieve and be grateful at the same time. One does not negate the other.

The parents of several children feel grateful for *all* their children, of course, and so they grieve deeply at the loss of any one of them. A spouse married for many years can look back fondly over decades of love yet still hurt terribly over the absence of his or her partner.

And so we give up comparisons. We don't compare our loss to the good things in our lives. We grieve the one and thank God for the others. Accepting this reality also frees people to be themselves and not try to "replace" a lost loved one. If one person has gone, we do not ask another to become a carbon copy of the absent one.

God does not replace our individual loss. He does not bring our loved one back to live with us. But He walks with us through healing and blesses us with newness of life and fresh relationships.

I HAVE NOTHING TO SAY TO GOD

As I was with Moses, so I will be with you; I will never leave you nor forsake you.
JOSHUA 1:5

"I try to talk with God or pray, but I can't," Marie said to me a number of months after her loss. She then told me that even though she had nothing to say to God, she would sit each morning in a particular chair in her living room and imagine herself sitting at the feet of Jesus. She would just sit, quietly, without any words forming in her mind.

Marie knew that the Lord was with her, despite her feelings. Even when anger consumed her, she came to her chair and sat in the presence of the Lord. Her mind swam with too much doubt — doubt about her ability to speak coherently and doubt about how God would respond — to even shape words out of her jumbled thoughts. But at the same time, she didn't want to stray too far from the presence of the Lord.

Of course, she didn't have to sit in a particular chair to come into His presence, but that distinction helped her separate all the other moments of her day from the moments at His feet.

God ably handles all of our emotions. He invites us to come to Him honestly and openly, trusting that He knows the pain of our hearts and that the Holy Spirit will correctly interpret our desires. But what happens when we have nothing to say, when we turn a cold shoulder to our available Lord?

I think that Marie's decision to sit in the presence of Jesus even though she had nothing to say showed a willingness to remain near Him and, perhaps, a tacit belief that He would touch her heart and open her mouth. You might say that her anger at God didn't move her to stomp off in disdain.

God does handle all of our emotions, but He also deserves our respect whenever we communicate with Him. Respect doesn't mean that we approach Him in cringing fear. Respect means that we demonstrate our knowledge and belief that God is still God. He is our loving Father, but He is also the Creator of the world, the Alpha and Omega, the great Jehovah. Words fail us when we try to wrap them around a description of God.

And so when Marie sat before God, she assumed a posture of respect. She felt too upset to speak, but she sat quietly at His feet. She did not act like a child throwing a tantrum but like a broken daughter waiting with her Father for enough healing to move her back into fellowship with Him.

Over time that healing did come, and Marie regained her desire to talk with the Lord. She opened up and spilled out all her pent-up emotions, her questions, and her fears. And God's love poured down into her soul, restoring reciprocal communion.

WHY DID THIS HAPPEN TO ME?

Now we see but a poor reflection as in a mirror; then we shall see face to face.
Now I know in part; then I shall know fully, even as I am fully known.

1 CORINTHIANS 13:12

Who among us hasn't felt a pang of sadness when viewing television reports of human suffering all over the world? Wars rage in the streets of Jerusalem, youths killing youths, parents wailing in the anguish of losing a child to stray bullets or suicide bombers.

Sometimes we witness devastation due to nature's wrath: flooding towns and villages or earthquakes leveling cities. We gasp or sigh and offer a prayer for those pierced by such heartache.

The faces of starving children, eyes dimmed to their true situation, cause us to shed a tear or even write a check. We want to help boys and girls in third world countries who face hardships we can't even begin to imagine.

We sincerely feel concern and sorrow for those less fortunate than we are. Compassion fills our hearts and often motivates us to do something for them, to alleviate their pain. Many ministries contribute greatly to the poor or victimized of the world, and we often contribute to those ministries.

Then we lose a loved one, and the experience of our own

suffering transforms our general concern into a piercing, personal reality. We are now the bereaved. The pain of loss leads us to cry out in our spirits, *Why did this happen to me? I never expected this. I'm not like the people I've watched on the evening news who suffer great tragedy.*

But we are. It seems incredible that death could invade the sanctity of our own family, and yet the absence of our loved one testifies to our vulnerability, our inability to escape what once seemed a faraway darkness.

In the past, we've been able to accept, with true feelings of sadness, that terrible things happen all the time. But that acceptance came with the unspoken denial that our lives would ever endure such pain. We may have never given a second thought to our own vulnerability while watching the nightly news and its recounting of each day's tragedies. We feel safe in our family rooms, sipping hot chocolate and headed to the comfort of soft beds inside houses protected by burglar alarms. We even feel it somehow unhealthy to focus on potential suffering.

But when loss does come, our very security contributes to the shock we feel. It seemed like this kind of pain happened to *other* people. It seemed more general than personal.

No longer.

Now we are part of the worldwide community of those who have suffered the loss of a loved one. Death favors no one. People of wealth and poverty alike fall victim. Those who live in ravaged lands and those who live in abundance all eventually face the end of life on this side of heaven.

What has happened to us happens to everyone — until the

Lord returns. It is the terrible result of living in a fallen world.

Thankfully, death does not write the final chapter for those who believe. The poor reflection we see now of God, and our limited understanding of why painful things happen to us, will one day be made clear. We will see God face-to-face. Our understanding will be complete and our pain will be over. And we will be home.

THE TROUBLE WITH SMALLER HOLIDAYS

Do not conform any longer to the pattern of this world, but be transformed by the renewing of your mind.

ROMANS 12:2

Jim and Annie moved through their Sunday-morning routine like they would on any other Sunday. Over coffee and cereal, Annie commented on the silence that echoed in the house since their toddler, Jimmy, had died. The very air seemed heavy even though the sun streamed in through the kitchen window.

More than ten months had elapsed, and the established routine on Sunday included church attendance, even on mornings when they would have preferred to remain alone with each other. But their church community had rallied around them, and the worship service often lifted the load of loss, if only for a few hours.

This June morning felt different, somehow. Father's Day has a way of doing that.

This was Jim's first Father's Day without his only child. He and Annie had talked about it the Sunday before as a flurry of newspaper and TV ads enticed buyers to avail themselves of bargain prices on ties and aftershave. They had decided to continue their routine and go to church, come home for a light lunch, and relax at home.

Now as they left the house, the thought of seeing so many little children streaming to church with a hand tucked safely in the grip of a father's protection loomed large. Jim and Annie made their way through the crowded narthex, greeting friends with smiles and waves. They sat down with a sense of relief that the worst was over.

Then as the pastor started to talk about Father's Day, tiny beads of sweat popped up on Jim's forehead. He knew what was coming, but he didn't know what to do. Should he rise when the pastor called for all fathers to stand? Could he handle the round of applause acknowledging this important role of any man with children? Jim had had only one child, and that child was gone. He had been a father but wasn't any longer.

Or was he? Annie squeezed his hand and nodded an affirmation that spoke volumes. Of course he was still a father. His loss did not negate the short years that his son lived with them. And certainly it did not negate the reality that his son still lived. He was in a better place but alive — eternally alive!

When Jim heard the pastor call for all fathers to stand up, he stood proudly with the other fathers. A trace of a bittersweet smile touched his lips. The moment had surprised him, but it soon passed. He had made a choice that affirmed his feelings of fatherhood, feelings so close to the surface on this morning of a holiday that until today hadn't seemed so big. He'd loved Father's Day the year of Annie's pregnancy and the ones following when they had celebrated at home with presents and a cake.

But this Father's Day had crept up on them and taken them emotionally by surprise. More "significant" holidays, such as Christmas, appeared on everyone's calendar, and weeks of preparation included plans with friends and family. But no one had even mentioned Father's Day.

That's the way it is with some holidays that pass quickly with little fuss. The feelings of deepened loss surprise us. And people around us often can't imagine such feelings. But as we move through the months and years of loss, we learn to think differently about holidays, just as we learn to think differently about all of life.

Special memories of our loved one touch us on holidays. It may be the smell of barbecued hamburgers on a grill on Memorial Day or the crackle of fireworks on the Fourth of July. We remember just what our loved one would have eaten or how he or she would have responded to the burst of a light show in the sky. And as we remember, we live in the present moment as well. It's a blend of the past and the present — with the hope of a reunited future.

'TIS THE SEASON

And the star they had seen in the east went ahead of them until it stopped over the place where the child was. When they saw the star, they were overjoyed.

MATTHEW 2:9-10

Two of the most celebrated holidays of the year stretch over weeks and fill the air with the excitement and festivity of a season of joy. I know that a lot of people find this season too commercial to enjoy, but I always loved it. I loved the warmth of added lights and the bustle of selecting gifts, preparing food, and designing activities to bring friends and family together.

But loss changes all of that. The empty place at the holiday table becomes the focal point of the meal. The presents *not* purchased stack up in the mind as the shopper passes by item after item. The music of the season, filling the air of every store for weeks before Christmas, brings tears to the eyes of those who have lost a loved one. We might wish we could just go to sleep on the day before Thanksgiving and wake up the day after New Year's.

For the first two years after Jack died, we celebrated Christmas in much the same way that we always had. I felt frustrated about having so much to do and didn't want to bother my friends, who seemed as busy as I was.

I remember one particularly troublesome afternoon when my attempts to "do it on my own" failed. The girls and I had purchased a Christmas tree and driven home with it tied to the roof of the car. Once home, I needed to get the tree off and into the house. I had no idea that a Christmas tree weighs as much as it does. Lisa and Lara tried to help me, but their arms couldn't even reach the trunk without branches scraping their faces. Dragging the tree instead of carrying it, I finally bullied it into the living room. Pine needles trailed all along the front walkway, entry, and living room floor. The next day I tried by myself to put the tree into a stand. Futile! Eventually I appealed to the sweet lady next door, and together we got it up.

When Christmas rolled around the next year, we branched out in a completely different direction — and never regretted it. I had wrongly assumed that Lisa and Lara would feel upset at any change in the routine. Delight shone on both of their faces when I told them we would be taking a trip over the Christmas holiday. My parents also responded excitedly when I asked if we could celebrate with them a week early. Because we would be gone for two weeks, we didn't even put up a tree — a tradition that ranks (almost) as a holy event for me. My mother fixed a full turkey dinner on the appointed day, and we opened presents around my parents' tree. Because the trip was our gift, our gifts to each other were small and few.

We had a truly wonderful time away that year and came back realizing that making changes can be healthy. Only that year alone did we forego a tree, and only that year did we go away, but it was good timing and the right choice.

Feel free to make changes that will help your own family better enjoy the biggest holiday season of the year. Yes, things will be different -- but they can still be good.

THE FICKLENESS OF TIME

Perseverance must finish its work so that you may be mature and complete, not lacking anything.

JAMES 1:4

For many years, I thought of a year as running from one September to another September. My birthday coincided with each school year's start, making September a month of beginnings for me. Contrary to fall's signal of dying, my life revved up. A fresh start in classes meant an opportunity to achieve better grades than the year before and a new social season brimming with possibilities.

I continued to mentally mark the passing of a year from September to September even after school years drifted into the past. Summer always moved along at a more leisurely pace than the other nine months of the year, and the New Year marked a holiday in the middle of my own calendar year. I seemed more inspired to make resolutions to change as September rolled around than on January 1, when the rest of the world started life over again.

Then Jack died.

My mental calendar shifted from September to December 15. One year since he died . . . two years . . . three . . . four. It's now been almost twenty-four years. December 15 is not a date, however, when I make resolutions or start things over. It is a day when I reflect on all that has changed since Jack left and when I thank God for His provision in the reality of my loss.

I remember, too, how people talked of the "magic" of passing the one-year mark after his death, as if grieving would conclude and normalcy would return. Who ever came up with the idea that a year is an adequate measure of healing? It had to be someone who had never lost a loved one.

One popular belief insists that living through all the days, anniversaries, and special events of one calendar year means immunity to future pain. By then you will have faced that first wedding anniversary with no partner or Christmas without a beloved child or Memorial Day without your father, and all will be well.

But then the second year after your loss rolls around, and the pain pierces almost as much as it did the year before. You do feel better, but loss still dominates your feelings. People around you, however, act as if the cure has taken hold and the sun shines in all its strength. Time has healed your wound.

But time *doesn't* heal; Jesus does. Of course, He works in the context of our time here on earth, but His timing seldom matches our own. Healing comes more quickly for some than for others. A multitude of factors contribute to each individual's movement from consuming grief to stability and wholeness.

Sometimes discouragement drags us down when we fail to progress as fast as we had anticipated. We look around and the world seems to go on as it did before our loved one left us — but we don't function at full speed at all. We still limp along with hurting hearts and watches that seem to have frozen on the day our loved departed.

Don't despair. Persevere. Keep getting up and keep taking one step at a time. No magic number of years exists by which you can measure your healing. Even so, restoration will happen if you stay close to Jesus. He will touch you again and again, and one day you will realize that the past year really did feel whole, fresh, and new.

CHURCH CAN BE SO PAINFUL

*I know what it is to be in need, and I know what it is to have plenty. I have
learned the secret of being content in any and every situation, whether well fed or
hungry, whether living in plenty or in want. I can do everything through him
who gives me strength.*

PHILIPPIANS 4:12-13

The day after Jack died in the hot-air-balloon accident, our pastor
delivered a powerful sermon about Jack and the two men killed
with him. The other two men and their families attended our same
church, so the accident was not only a personal loss but also a community one.

Literally hundreds of people supported us in countless ways.
Many brought meals, some came over and cleaned our house, one
man took care of the lawn and yard work, others helped with business decisions, and so very many wrote notes that provided comfort for me and the girls for months after Jack died. That
community of believers went above and beyond any expectation I
could have had of how help would come in the midst of our loss.

For many Sundays, I felt as though everyone around me was
reaching out to us. We remained the center of attention and heard
carefully chosen words about husbands and fathers and death and

loss. Church became a place of safety, and we felt as if we belonged there more than anywhere else.

As the weeks turned into months, however, the focus at church appropriately shifted away from the accident to the more routine issues of everyday life: how to live with tight finances, what a particular Bible passage means to us today, how to rear children, how families should live as followers of Jesus, how husbands and wives should relate.

More and more, I began to feel like an outsider. So many lessons focused on the nuclear family: mom, dad, and the kids. Singleness seemed alien to the culture of the pew. Before Jack died I had never noticed this family focus. Suddenly, the natural vocabulary of Sunday morning became abrasive to my ears. As I looked around, I saw many other people like me — people who had lost a loved one and therefore no longer fit the definition of a normal family.

During a sermon about how husbands should treat their wives, I'd noticed a woman sitting alone and wondered what she was thinking. Another time — as the children's choir filed out, evoking laughter and applause — I watched a parent who had recently lost a child. The very normal behavior of Sunday morning stung many who now sat in pews where their loved one had sat just weeks or months before.

At other moments during a church service, I sensed a closeness to God that felt consuming. Distractions ceased, and heaven descended into the sanctuary. The distance between the spiritual world and the earthly world shrank to nothing, and joy filled every corner of the room. The mere mention of heaven in a song opened the floodgates and tears of longing spilled out. Death was conquered, and praises of God's people rose beyond the rooftop.

In those moments of spiritual bliss, the secret of contentment revealed itself. The reality of Jesus and what He did for all who believe in Him pushed out the pain of alienation. It didn't matter if everyone fit the description of the examples in the sermon. We were all together as the body of Christ, praising Him and experiencing moments of transformation. Contentment filled our hearts, and we felt renewed to face another week.

And so it can be for you.

I NEVER THOUGHT LIFE WOULD BE LIKE THIS

By faith Abraham, when called to go to a place he would later receive as his inheritance, obeyed and went, even though he did not know where he was going.

HEBREWS 11:8

I like to look way ahead into the future and make plans. Before one vacation ends, I check on travel deals and dates to see where we can go next. My Daytimer holds calendars for several years to come, along with the pages for this year. Lists fill my purse and schedules shape each day.

I've learned that these plans of mine often get interrupted or changed. They are not set in concrete, and at any moment I need to be ready to turn in an unexpected direction.

I hadn't yet learned that lesson when Jack died. My plan called for us to live the proverbial "grow old together" kind of life and die at a ripe old age. Jack's insurance business would continue to grow, and I would remain at home with our children as they grew up. They would marry and live near me, and I would be Super Nana. I had no plan B.

When the immediate shock of our loss lessened, I woke up one day and thought, *What do I do now?* Up to that point, my mind and emotions had functioned from moment to moment. The girls and I measured life day to day. Then healing began to make room for new insights and new plans for the future, and I realized that I needed to change my thinking.

I wouldn't be growing old with Jack, his insurance business was closing, and my children needed me to be their mother at home *and* their provider in the world. Thinking about them marrying and my future days as a grandmother drifted far away into a future I couldn't imagine.

A process began to unfold that would become part of my life for a long time. It began with acceptance of life as it had become. I would have liked it to be different, but it wasn't.

I started to pray specifically for guidance about everything. I clung to every word I read in the Bible as if it were the life-preserver that it really is. The faith that Abraham had when he left his home and headed into the unknown became the faith I now embraced. I didn't know how to plan for the future. I didn't know what God had in mind for us now that Jack was gone.

And so I prayed and read the Bible. I talked with people about different options regarding finances, work, care of the children, and every aspect of our lives. It became clear to me that God would not unfold a scroll of my life and give me the big picture. Oh, I knew that we would all reunite in heaven some day, but I didn't know what would happen during the days until then.

At first, the daunting task of gathering information threatened me. I called on a lot of people for help in deciphering legal papers and setting up filing systems to manage our household. After a while, the tasks became almost fun. I felt a sense of accomplishment when I learned a new skill.

I came to understand that faith involved both a reliance on God and a forward movement on my part. The movement didn't have to take me very far — just to the next step. Just as God walked with Abraham all along the way of his journey, He walked all along the way of mine.

He walks with you, too. By faith you can begin to sculpt a new life that works despite your loved one's absence. Life unfolds differently than you expected, but God is with you as you move through it. He will give you direction, at least for the next step. Instead of a well-laid-out plan, a new adventure awaits. Although the pain of loss remains with you, you move forward in the faith of your forefathers, not knowing what yet lies ahead. But you keep moving forward anyway.

REMEMBERING THE DAY

I thank my God every time I remember you.

PHILIPPIANS 1:3

The first anniversary of Jack's death drew close. I didn't know how we should spend the day or what would be best for Lisa and Lara. Of all the commemorative days that had passed that year, this one seemed the most significant. It marked the absence of our loved one that resulted in the change in our lives.

I didn't want to cause the children to feel sad all day, but I knew we had to do something special. Oddly enough, I don't remember exactly what we did. I know we were together, and I know many of our friends sent cards or called. What I do remember is the awareness, after that first anniversary, that we would face December 15 every year for the rest of our lives.

While the girls were still young and at home, we spent the day together. The morning of each anniversary, we prayed together, remembered Jack, cried a little, and maybe spent time with friends later in the day. As Lisa and Lara got older, their school schedules filled up with sports and other activities, adding a sense of normalcy to December 15. The significance of the day remained, but we didn't alter our routines to commemorate it.

Then Lisa went away to college. That year I began to think about some way to express our mutual loss when distance prevented us from being together. I wanted something more than a phone call but also something that we could repeat as the years went by and lifestyles changed. Maybe we would all live in the same area again, or we might be fanned out across the globe.

I finally decided to send each daughter a dozen sweetheart roses every year on December 15. That way they would receive something beautiful, no matter where they lived or what they were doing. Today they are both busy mothers of young children. Lisa lives nearby, and Lara lives several states away. We talk by phone on December 15, and they know that a dozen roses will arrive sometime that day.

We live out our remembering in the context of our everyday lives. We each thank God for the years we had Jack and then go about the day as usual. Remembering Jack and remembering to thank God for the time we had with him infuses this anniversary with God's love and comfort.

As you move through the days of your loss, you will face your own anniversaries. You and those close to you will have the opportunity to commemorate the day in a way that meaningfully meets each of your needs. Your family's unique desires will shape how the day unfolds.

The early anniversary days feel painful, but as time goes on and healing takes place, the anniversary of your loved one's death changes from a day of darkness into a day of bittersweet light. Heaven becomes more and more real, and God's love wraps you in His comfort.

When I send the roses to my daughters, the card reads the same every year. I use a simple word that sums up what that day has come to mean and what we do on it. I sign it,

Remembering,
Love, Mom.

WHEN ANXIETY FEELS OVERWHELMING

Cast all your anxiety on him because he cares for you.

1 PETER 5:7

Water poured in torrents over the windshield. I gripped the wheel of the car and slowed down to a crawl. I didn't want to stop altogether because other cars might have been behind me. Two of my grandsons, Justin and Alex, sat in the backseat, screaming in unison as visibility dropped to zero.

I had picked up the boys at school, and we were driving to their home during a thunderous storm. Streets overflowed with rushing water, and streams poured down each side of the road. I'd pulled off the highway to a smaller road, only to face huge sprays of water careening over our car as others passed me.

Between the waves that washed over the windshield, we sang and laughed to break the tension of the drive. Justin and Alex expressed amazement at how fast the rain fell. By the time we arrived at their house, impressions marked the palms of my hands from my tight grip on the wheel. Lisa opened the garage door and waved us in with a big smile.

Although I never felt that we were in any real danger, the sense of overwhelming circumstances growing around us did raise the adrenaline level in us all. If we had driven much farther, I know the strain would have increased.

Anxiety in your soul after the loss of a loved one can have the same swamping impact. You know intellectually that you are in no real danger but still you feel overwhelmed. You can't see beyond the next moment. As more and more demands fall on you, you slow the pace of your life to a crawl.

Like our car caught in the tumultuous weather, you can't get away. The reality of your situation surrounds you and consumes your emotions. You grip tightly to any semblance of stability and comfort.

What can help subdue the rising tide of anxiety and guide you through the flood of feelings? Only an awareness of God's presence. Slowing down and breathing deeply reduces your sense of fear. You can hum, smile, relax your grip on your imagination, and regain your composure.

When anxiety feels overwhelming, invite others into your experience. While I felt responsible for Justin and Alex as I drove in the storm, their presence comforted me. They expressed amazement at the power of the circumstances and laughed, albeit nervously, at the raging storm outside.

Consider calling a friend and admitting your feelings. Just talking with someone who cares about you lessens the anxiety. If it doesn't, ask for help. Ask someone to come over and just be with you. Take a break from your usual activity and focus on what you know to be true.

While driving the car, I had said to myself, *Only a few more miles, only a few more miles.* You can repeat any number of verses to give you comfort. Take in the truth and lean on Jesus. Cast all your anxiety on Him, for He cares for you.

No One Feels Like I Do

For we do not have a high priest who is unable to sympathize with our weaknesses, but we have one who has been tempted in every way, just as we are—yet was without sin. Let us then approach the throne of grace with confidence, so that we may receive mercy and find grace to help us in our time of need.

HEBREWS 4:15-16

"Oh, I know just how you feel."

These familiar words fall often upon the ears of those of us who have lost a loved one. Sometimes the person speaking does know how we feel, especially if he or she also has lost a loved one. Even then, it's difficult for us to comprehend that anyone could feel our pain or understand the alienation that separates us from the world around us.

I remember shopping for a new bed soon after Jack died. We'd shared a water bed that he loved and I disliked immensely. In those days, water beds had no adjustments for the imbalances created by varying weight distribution. Jack would lie down, and I would pop up on top of a mound of displaced water. After he died, I couldn't face crawling back into that bed alone, knowing that I would have gladly endured any discomfort just to have him next to me.

And so I found myself standing in a mattress showroom, staring at rows of beds designed to accommodate two people. Tears welled up in my eyes as I turned away from the approaching salesclerk. This sudden rush of emotion surprised me. Feelings of awkwardness grew inside me as I stood in a sea of glaring reality: Our world overflows with couples. Singles often feel they're on the outside looking in.

I imagine similar feelings overwhelm those who have lost a child when they see school-crossing signs or "Baby on Board" bumper stickers. Pain unexpectedly pierces them, and the "normal" world feels alien.

No matter who you've lost, you experience the strangeness of living in the world without your loved one. As people around you seem to effortlessly go about their business — working, playing, running errands, going to the movies, eating out — you wonder how the world can keep turning as if all is well.

I wanted to scream at the salesclerk in the mattress store, "I'm a widow! A widow! I sleep alone! Do you realize how I feel in this store of big beds?" Of course, I said none of that. I choked down the words, smiled, and bought a queen-size bed. The few twin beds in the back of the showroom looked too forlorn for me to even consider.

We can receive great comfort when someone who's suffered a similar loss reaches out to us. But even then, we each experience loss individually. On a human level, no one feels like you do.

On a spiritual level, however, we have someone who closely identifies with our loss. Christ truly does know how you feel. He has suffered as you do and, in fact, bore the greater pain of alienation when He was crucified for the sins of the world.

"The sins of the world" must seem like a remote doctrinal phrase as you live in the midst of personal loss. But the pain that Christ endured put Him on a level with all of us. He isn't an aloof high priest, removed from us and exempt from the pain we suffer.

And because He is divine, the comfort He offers has supernatural power to touch your hurting heart with His love. He doesn't give you words intended to erase your pain, but He invites you to come confidently to Him and bring your grief. He sits on a throne of grace, and He welcomes you with open arms. He hurts for you and with you.

Release the feelings you hide as you walk in the world, where your loss often goes unnoticed by others in the rush of everyday life. Christ is in no rush. He has time for you and offers understanding far surpassing that of any other.

PEOPLE CAN SAY THE DUMBEST THINGS

Let your gentleness be evident to all.

PHILIPPIANS 4:5

"I can't believe she said that!" the young woman barked in exasperation. "She told me to be glad that I have other children."

Mary and her husband had recently lost a child to a fatal illness and now faced the world of well-meaning, but often poorly speaking, people.

I remember going to church one Sunday and being greeted by a woman in the hallway. Jack had been gone for several months, and I'd attended church regularly during that time. This woman had seen me, and apparently my demeanor had annoyed her.

She took me by the shoulders and actually shook me.

"You have to cry!" she yelled. "You have to cry!"

I looked at her in shock and amazement. She walked away as I watched her with my mouth wide open. I immediately started a voiceless conversation in my mind defending my public behavior.

I cry a lot! I weep buckets into steaming bubble baths; I pace in the middle of the night in tears; I cry at home with friends and my children! I silently shouted to the woman still present in my mind.

For many months I felt resentment every time I thought about this woman. I avoided her when I saw her coming and repeated the details of our encounter to my friends.

Anyone who has lost a loved one has experienced similar insensitivity. A familiar verse, Romans 8:28, often gets quoted to the grieving. You know, "All things work together for good."

People don't mean to be hurtful; they just don't know what to say. They can't imagine why quoting Scripture might engender wrath. They don't see that words meant to change our feelings imply that the pain of loss can be treated with a Band-Aid.

While the truth of Scripture is no Band-Aid, the delivery of it often is. A word in passing feels like a quick fix: "Just believe this and you will be healed." Of course, we believe wholeheartedly that "all things work together for good," but that reality takes time for us to internalize. And it doesn't mean that the good comes without pain.

The family who lost a child loves their other children. They feel grateful for them. But the presence of the others does not erase the loss of the missing one.

So what do we do about insensitive people?

We forgive them. We respond gently to them. I had to learn this over and over and eventually had to apply this teaching to the shoulder-shaking woman. I stopped avoiding her and talking about her to others. She never became a good friend, but we learned to be cordial to each other.

Huge discomfort motivates people to put their feet in their mouths. They can't imagine how painful it must be to lose a loved one, so they struggle to say a kind word. That word often comes out crosswise and hurts us.

In the early days of loss, our gentleness may lie buried beneath consuming pain. But with healing, we can learn to gently forgive.

REMINDERS OF GOD'S GOODNESS

When the whole nation had finished crossing the Jordan, the Lord said to Joshua,
"Choose twelve men from among the people, one from each tribe, and tell them to
take up twelve stones from the middle of the Jordan from right where the priests
stood and to carry them over with you and put them down at the place where you
stay tonight."

JOSHUA 4:1-3

When pain consumes our thoughts, we might find it difficult to
remember God's goodness. The greater the pain, the longer we
struggle to find relief. Physical, emotional, spiritual, relational
pain — they all debilitate us. Just when we need our faith the most,
we may find it difficult to appropriate it.

The account of the Israelites as they prepared to cross the
Jordan illustrates one biblical situation in which fearful circumstances gripped the people of God. Even though the previous
generation of Israelites had lived through the parting of the Red
Sea when they fled from Pharaoh's army, this new generation must
have felt a familiar rush of apprehension as they looked upon the
flood-level Jordan.

Yet they obeyed Joshua and crossed, once again, through
parted waters on dry land and came up on the other side into the

Promised Land. They must have felt tremendous relief. They had arrived at the end of a long journey and prepared to settle the land their God had provided for them. God then commanded Joshua:

> "Choose twelve men from among the people, one from each tribe, and tell them to take up twelve stones from the middle of the Jordan from right where the priests stood and to carry them over with you and put them down at the place where you stay tonight."
>
> So Joshua called together the twelve men he had appointed from the Israelites, one from each tribe, and said to them, "Go over before the ark of the LORD your God into the middle of the Jordan. Each of you is to take up a stone on his shoulder, according to the number of tribes of the Israelites, to serve as a sign among you. In the future, when your children ask you, 'What do these stones mean?' tell them that the flow of the Jordan was cut off before the ark of the covenant of the LORD. When it crossed the Jordan, the waters of the Jordan were cut off. These stones are to be a memorial to the people of Israel forever" (Joshua 4:1-7).

God knows that we are a forgetful people. When pain ceases and relief floods our souls, we can forget the miracle of God's grace that brought us through the difficult time. You may feel you will never reach a time when difficulty doesn't dog your every step, but it will come. You will never forget the loss of your loved one, but healing will give you relief and help you move forward. Memorials along the way can provide help.

Reminders or memorials need not be elaborate or even physical structures. They can be something as simple as a framed photo illustrating the goodness of God. It could be a picture of a child being baptized that brings to mind the movement of God in that child's heart. It could be a photo of a stunning sunset that reveals the power of God in the glory of His creation.

Certain verses may remind you of comfort in the midst of pain. The verses can be noted in a journal or displayed in some prominent place in the home.

It doesn't matter how you remind yourself of God's goodness, but it may prove helpful to make your own version of the twelve stones the Israelites placed on the other side of the Jordan — the side that bordered the Promised Land.

REALIZE YOU HAVE A CHOICE

Brothers, we do not want you to be ignorant about those who fall asleep, or to grieve like the rest of men, who have no hope.

1 THESSALONIANS 4:13

After a time of healing — different for each person — you will be ready to transition from shocked grief to hopeful movement. You will have absorbed the blow and welcomed God's healing touch into every pore of your being. You'll recognize this time when the good days stretch out longer than the bad days. The desire to live will seep back into your heart, and your motivation to get up and going will propel you forward.

Sometimes, however, you may feel tempted to remain paralyzed by your loss. Even when motivated, it takes great effort to reconstruct a life and reenter a world inhabited by people who don't seem to notice your pain. Feeling better might even seem threatening; it might mean that another big change lurks around the corner.

Remaining a victim may feel comfortable in a strange, almost passive way. You may truly have been a victim — someone who has suffered tremendous pain as a result of something you could not control. Why shouldn't you continue to grieve and rely on others to meet your needs? Because you do not "grieve like the rest of men, who have no hope." Death has been overcome; it is a defeated enemy. Yes, you must live with loss, but not the loss of those who don't know God. You have hope, not only for eternity but for the present. God wants to heal you and bless you.

You must choose whether you will stop living in a way defined by your loss or whether you will continue to view all of life as a result of that loss. After loss, we have a tendency to think that everything difficult that touches us touches us because of that loss.

After Jack died, Lisa and Lara would often say that the discipline they were about to receive would be different if their dad were still alive. For a while, I bought this normal childhood guilt trip. Then I realized that what they said really wasn't true. Jack had been a disciplinarian, too. He may have handled any given situation differently than I did, but the result would be the same: We would have trained our children to grow into responsible, godly adults.

So instead of wringing my hands and lamenting the absence of Jack's wisdom, I began to tell the girls that I was now the only parent they had and that I would do the best I could. They needed to obey me no matter how they felt about it.

Young children challenge all parental discipline. Convincing arguments abound from those about to suffer a consequence for disobedience. Lisa and Lara still sharply felt the loss of their father, but this was not the real reason they tried to get out of just punishment.

Our world is unfair. You will face much injustice as you move through life, and a lot of it will have nothing to do with your loss.

The way you handle difficulty may change because of your loss, but you are not a victim of the wrongs of this world. You are a child of God with a living hope in your relationship with your Father. The unconditional love of God will transform you when you choose to take hold of life and see what God has in store for you.

GOD WHISPERS IN THE WHIRLWIND

And after the fire came a gentle whisper.

1 KINGS 19:12

One Old Testament prophet must have felt much the way you feel. His circumstances differ from yours, but like you, his emotional resources felt strained almost to the breaking point. His story shows how God provided a place for rest and healing. Elijah served as a prophet during the time of Ahab, one of the most evil kings of Israel. God used Elijah to destroy the prophets of Baal, which greatly angered the wicked Queen Jezebel.

> *Now Ahab told Jezebel everything Elijah had done and how he had killed all the prophets with the sword. So Jezebel sent a messenger to Elijah to say, "May the gods deal with me, be it ever so severely, if by this time tomorrow I do not make your life like that of one of them."*
>
> *Elijah was afraid and ran for his life. When he came to Beersheba in Judah, he left his servant there, while he himself went a day's journey into the desert. He came to a broom tree, sat down under it and prayed that he might die. "I have had*

enough, LORD," he said. "Take my life. I am no better than
my ancestors." Then he lay down under the tree and fell asleep.

All at once an angel touched him and said, "Get up and
eat." He looked around, and there by his head was a cake of
bread baked over hot coals, and a jar of water. He ate and
drank and then lay down again.

The angel of the LORD came back a second time and
touched him and said, "Get up and eat, for the journey is too
much for you." So he got up and ate and drank. Strengthened
by that food, he traveled forty days and forty nights until he
reached Horeb, the mountain of God. There he went into a
cave and spent the night. (1 Kings 19:1-9)

In the beginning of this passage, we see Elijah afraid and
exhausted. He felt so upset that he asked God to take his life. At
times we all feel ready to give up—maybe not ready to die but
ready to quit. Certainly, loss can wear us out to the point of
despair. We need rest and the ministering touch that only God can
provide.

Elijah's sanctuary under the branches of the broom tree shel-
tered him while he rested. Angels administered the gifts of God to
him. And then the voice of God told him to go and stand in the
Lord's presence, for the Lord was about to pass by.

Elijah stood on the mountain and witnessed howling winds
that tore the mountain apart, a mighty earthquake, and a roaring
fire. In all of these displays of awesome power, Elijah looked for the
Lord but did not find Him. Then a gentle whisper came to Elijah's

ears: The voice of the Lord softly communed with him and told him what to do next (see 1 Kings 19:11-12).

You have been living in your own whirlwind, tossed about by the powerful forces of loss. Perhaps you've wondered where God is. How can you hear Him? How can you know what to do next?

Today God doesn't customarily appear to us the way He appeared to the prophets of the Old Testament, but we can still know that we are in the presence of the Lord. We can still sense His still, quiet voice in our spirits as we seek His comfort and guidance.

Take time in the midst of your own whirlwind to sit in quiet and listen. Clear your mind, calm your emotions, and ask the God of all creation to whisper to you.

HELP TO WITHSTAND TEMPTATION

Then he returned to his disciples and found them sleeping. "Could you men not keep watch with me for one hour?" he asked Peter.

MATTHEW 26:40

Jesus asked Peter a disturbing question in the Garden of Gethsemane: "Could you men not keep watch with me for one hour?" Pain consumed the Master beyond what any of us can imagine, and He wanted those closest to Him to be with Him. Yet while Jesus agonized about His coming ordeal, Peter and the others with him had fallen asleep.

Even Jesus wanted the comfort of loved ones in His time of anguish. He had asked them to "keep watch" with Him.

What were His friends supposed to be watching for while Jesus prayed? Because this scene took place just before Jesus' betrayal and arrest, we might assume they were to watch for the approaching enemy. Maybe, though, it's more than that. Maybe Jesus wanted them to help Him persevere in keeping the will of the Father.

Scripture tells us that Jesus said, "My soul is overwhelmed with sorrow to the point of death. Stay here and keep watch with me" (Matthew 26:38). His human nature and our own share a common vulnerability. He felt deeply distraught and, perhaps, the tug of some great temptation. Jesus asked the Father to take the cup from Him. In the garden, an internal struggle prompted Jesus to ask His loved ones to rally around Him and supply Him with some needed reinforcement. Despite the lack of help from His sleeping companions, Jesus resisted the lure of sin and submitted to God's will.

We, on the other hand, find sin and temptation harder to resist. Unlike Jesus, we are born with a propensity to sin. And we find our human frailty further weakened by the devastating ravages of loss. We often feel weary and long for relief from pain. With such vulnerability, temptation lurks bold and strong, just around the corner.

The first book I wrote, *The Snare: Understanding Emotional and Sexual Entanglements*, addresses this very issue. While this may seem like a strange topic for a book on loss, it is sadly very appropriate. After Jack died, I found that I had become a target for the wiles of the enemy in the most subtle ways. I didn't feel tempted to get drunk, go carousing, hurt anyone, or steal, but I did feel tempted to seek human comfort where available. Opportunities for emotional entanglements — relationships with married men — proved more accessible than one might expect, especially in the Christian community.

Unfortunately, we are all too familiar with stories of bereaved men and women who become involved with a married coworker, counselor, or pastor. Most of the time, these people didn't intend to fall to the temptation of an immoral relationship. They simply never understood their vulnerability to making poor choices; they weren't on "watch" for the enemy.

My own awareness led me to interview many women and men tempted in similar ways. Some had succumbed to the temptation; they deeply regretted their actions and wished they had been wiser. Many agreed that being in accountable relationships would have helped them make better choices. They could have benefited from someone to talk with when they felt weak, someone to ask them tough questions. Most of them didn't have those kinds of watchful relationships when they needed them.

We can look to Jesus in the garden as an example of our need for support. Although His support failed Him, He remained sinless. We need trusted people around us who won't fall asleep while we agonize over our loss.

TRANSCENDENT FAITH

Indeed, in our hearts we felt the sentence of death. But this happened that we might not rely on ourselves but on God, who raises the dead.

2 CORINTHIANS 1:9

The first chapter of 2 Corinthians tells about the sufferings Paul and those with him endured for the sake of the gospel. Paul referred to the province of Asia (modern-day Turkey) and the pressure he felt while there. He even feared that he might die. Paul thanked God for delivering them from death, but he knew that even death could not defeat them: Their faith in Christ would carry them from this world into the next, and eternal life would be their reward. They had hope in this life and beyond death as well.

Albert Camus once wrote, "The future is the only transcendental value for men without God." Wow! People without God have no hope beyond death. Once their future ends, hope disappears. Or if their future turns into a painful present, they suffer without any godly help.

The Resurrection testifies to the power of our God. No matter how horrible our present circumstances may seem, we trust a God who raised Christ from the dead and who raises all who trust in Him to eternal life. Our faith takes us above, or beyond, the valley of the shadow. Regardless of our future, we can look past this life and anticipate heaven.

What a wonderfully freeing feeling to know we do not have to rely on ourselves to make it through the difficulties of life! When we have lost a loved one, we certainly know our limitations. We could not keep them here with us, and we cannot navigate the future on our own resources. Yet we also know the rest we can enjoy when we abandon ourselves to God and His unconditional love.

The Lord meets us in our need and restores us to wholeness as His power transforms our futures into hopeful tomorrows instead of dreaded dead ends. I grew up hearing stories about people who jumped out of high-rise windows when the stock market crashed in the 1930s. It seemed incomprehensible to me that anything could cause such a hopeless reaction.

But the loss of a loved one can feel that devastating if our faith doesn't transcend death. If death means the end, then we have little to be hopeful about. Even if we and our loved ones could live to a ripe old age, the end eventually would come. The grave would claim all our hopes and bury them with our earthly bodies.

We who trust in Jesus have no such grim future. Life after death, based on God's grace and not our own good works, washes our souls in a hope that cannot be destroyed. The resurrection of Jesus guarantees our own resurrection — when we will enjoy eternal life in heaven with our loved ones and the Lord.

BEYOND OUR IMAGINATION

Now to him who is able to do immeasurably more than all we ask or imagine,
according to his power that is at work within us, to him be glory in the church and
in Christ Jesus throughout all generations, for ever and ever! Amen.

EPHESIANS 3:20-21

It was a beautiful Sunday afternoon, and our daughter Lisa, her husband, Chadd, and their son, Justin, were celebrating her birthday at our house. After dinner, Lisa hurried everyone out the front door for a brisk walk.

"I hope she won't be too disappointed," I said to her sister, Lara, as we took off in a group down the street. Lara smiled and nodded silently.

Lisa's motivation for the walk originated many years ago in her father's family. Jack and his two brothers all had the same birthday, although in different years. We always celebrated July 14 with a big party as the brothers and their families gathered for the joint birthday.

Lisa came into this world on July 13, just seven hours "early." She was due to arrive on July 4 but held on until the evening of July 13. Even at that, our family felt amazed at the close proximity to the famed July 14 date, so over the years, we had a joint birthday celebration for Lisa and Jack. When Jack died, she suffered a heart-breaking loss at each birthday party.

Lisa's second child was due eleven days after our brisk Sunday afternoon walk. She had been praying that he would be born on her dad's birthday, and she did all she could to move things along. She walked with arms swinging and talked optimistically about having the baby the next day, despite my warnings about being disappointed if he didn't arrive on her timetable.

As they left our house that evening, Chadd hugged me and said, "Well, Mom, I'll be calling you in a few hours." We both smiled and passed a knowing glance, as if to dismiss Lisa's futile attempts.

A few hours later, the phone rang and roused me out of a deep sleep. The numbers on the digital clock next to our bed glowed brightly, wordlessly announcing the hour: 12:05 AM — on July 14!

"Hello," I said, with the sudden alertness of a grandmother knowing she is very shortly headed to the hospital.

"Hi, Mom," Chadd said in a voice filled with irony. "As I came up to bed and our clock turned over to midnight, Lisa's water broke. We are getting ready to go to the hospital right away."

I asked the Lord to forgive my unbelief as I pulled on sweats and gathered up my packed suitcase for the days ahead to be spent at home with the growing family.

I drove the empty roads to the hospital, smiling all the way at the goodness of God to answer Lisa's prayer. She had a full twenty-four hours to deliver a baby and still hit her dad's birthday!

At around 4 AM, Jackson Alexander Miller was born. His Grandpa-Jack-in-heaven must have been peeking over the clouds of heaven with both hands gesturing in a thumbs-up salute at the birth of his second grandchild.

All of us, including Lisa, would have felt delighted with Alex's birth no matter what day he arrived. We would have sympathized with Lisa that this particular wish didn't come true, but it would have been a small disappointment on the larger scale of life.

God, however, had something else in mind. He decided to pour out this special blessing on our family, like icing on a cake. We give Him all the credit and dismiss the doctor's explanation that babies are born early in Colorado due to the altitude. That seems to be true, but we know that this little boy was born early because God answered the prayer of a little girl who lost her dad (and her birthday partner) many years ago. As a grown woman, she now celebrates with her son, and we continue to thank God for bringing a blessing to us beyond our imagination.

This extraordinary blessing enlarged my faith. It brought a smile to my face as I thought of God's delight in pouring out His love on Lisa in this way. And I began to believe that it really is okay with Him when His children ask for things they want but don't really need. Of course, those things need to be consistent with Scripture and with His will, but they don't need to only be the necessities of life.

Enlarge your own faith. Ask God for what is on your heart. If you don't receive your request, ask God for the grace to receive His will. If, on the other hand, He does grant your request, you will bask in the wonder of His touch that went way beyond your imagination.

QUESTION MARKS

Hear, O LORD, and answer me, for I am poor and needy.

PSALM 86:1

We want answers! Racing our nimble fingers across the keyboards of home computers, we access information at dizzying speeds and in enormous quantities. One query in the search box on the Google website can elicit hundreds, if not thousands, of responses.

We can fall into the same pattern spiritually when life doesn't make sense to us. *Why Lord?* We often demand an immediate answer from the God of the universe. We study the Bible in courses like systematic theology, imagining that we can organize Scripture in ways that logically explain most of its teachings. Christian books abound to help us rationally understand and maneuver through the pages of Scripture in ways that answer life's toughest questions.

It is often difficult for us as twenty-first-century Christians to accept that some things are unknowable. Suspicion may even creep into our thinking when we face unsuitable answers to our questions. Sometimes we feel the need to construct an answer by manipulating Scripture to suit our point of view, determined to make God make sense.

The word *mystery* has largely dropped out of the evangelical vocabulary. Sometimes we avoid it because of potential dubious associations. Strains of new-age music often cling to a word found on the pages of Scripture, and we fear to reflect on mystery because a vagrant spirituality has also claimed it.

But Scripture tells us that God is a God of mystery. Job 11:7 says, "Can you fathom the mysteries of God? Can you probe the limits of the Almighty?" Revelation 10:7 tells us that a day will come when "the mystery of God will be accomplished."

Certainly, the loss of a loved one pushes questions from deep within our souls right up to the surface of our minds and hearts. Why did our loved one die? Why didn't God prevent it? Why, God, why?

At Jack's memorial service, a number of people came to know the Lord. I heard of several who even prayed to accept Christ in the parking lot of the church after the service. I consider those conversions wonderful blessings that came out of a tragedy.

But I have to admit that if God had given me the option of saving those people or having Jack live, I would have chosen Jack's life. I feel grateful that his death brought glory to God and resulted in souls finding eternal life, but I also believe that God was, and is, big enough that He could have turned those people's hearts to Him in some other way.

I can also very pragmatically say that Jack died as the result of an accident consistent with the way our world works: The balloon hit power lines, resulting in a catastrophic fire that caused his death.

Again, the possible answer to the *Why?* question seems less than satisfactory. When it comes to death, we think accidents shouldn't happen. Perhaps you have lost a loved one to a disease that invaded a healthy body, unseen and without apparent reason. Silent, pervasive killers live in the air we breathe and take human life without apparent discrimination.

We are able to live with unanswered questions only when we fully trust the God we serve. Aspects of Him remain a mystery. His ways are not our ways. Still, we do know that He loves us uncondi-tionally and will work all of life out for our good. We may not be able to see that working out, but it is in full swing.

Websites and computer programs can't give us answers to our deepest questions. We simply must lay them down at the foot of the cross and thank God for His love, despite our inability to com-prehend what He is doing.

THE DWELLING PLACE OF GOD

How lovely is your dwelling place,
O LORD Almighty!
My soul yearns, even faints,
for the courts of the Lord;
my heart and my flesh cry out
for the living God.

PSALM 84:1-2

The Israeli soldier stepped in front of Steve and held a machine gun out in front of him.

"You can go no farther," he said sternly.

We had ascended steps at the end of a dark tunnel stretching from the Muslim section of the Old City of Jerusalem to the entrance of Temple Mount, the area where the temple stood in the time of Jesus. That temple, considered one of the architectural masterpieces of its day, went up in flames in AD 70 when the Romans put the torch to it. Its destruction marked a tremendous loss to the world, and not just to the Jewish and Christian populations.

Today, on the thirty-five acres of Temple Mount stands the third-holiest mosque in the Muslim world and the brilliant, golden Dome of the Rock. The whole area has been closed to the public for several years now ever since violence erupted in the fall of 2000. One of the world's most impressive and holy places has become the center of a raging war yet unsettled.

In January 2001, Steve and I found ourselves at the barred entrance to Temple Mount. Steve's journalistic spirit drew him to the confrontation with the gun-toting soldier like a moth to a flame, while my enthusiasm paled as we entered the tunnel. This dark, cavernous passageway revealed little of the bustling trade center it had been just months before. Local merchants had sold their wares to eager tourists going to and from Temple Mount. Only two stands still occupied the tunnel. In one, an elderly Muslim man brewed Turkish coffee, and in the other, three Muslim men displayed their beaded necklaces and other trinkets for sale.

Steve pleaded with the soldier, asking to just peek through the partially open door and take a picture of the Dome of the Rock. The solider stepped closer to Steve with a look of stern determination that sent me sailing down the steps, calling to Steve to hurry up and come with me.

Later that day, we stopped at an elaborate model of Jerusalem during the time of Jesus. The temple shines in all its splendor. Elegant pillars surround the courtyard, and beautiful tiles enhance many facades of the building. Miniature palm trees cast cool shadows, even in their model setting.

As I looked at the model temple, I could just imagine what it must have been like to live during that time and go to the place where God dwelt with His people. We read much about the temple in the Old Testament, and other detailed accounts describe its exquisite beauty.

Psalm 84 is attributed to a temple assistant barred from the temple by conquerors. His words convey the power and comfort that the people of Israel experienced in the House of God. In the "courts of the LORD," the writer himself enjoyed spiritual renewal.

How blessed we are that the presence of the Lord lives within us. By inviting Jesus into our lives, we receive the Holy Spirit and bask in God's presence all the time. We are not bound to one site, one physical place, where we can meet with God.

The cares of the world may press in on us and cause us to forget that we dwell with Him, but He is present. Often, we can sense His presence more acutely when we go to church and sit with other believers in a peaceful setting where we focus expressly on the Lord.

Wherever we are, what an amazing privilege we have to relax in the presence of the living God and know that one day we will enjoy even more of His presence in heaven. The beauty of the temple here on earth will seem a distant and shadowy memory dwarfed by the eternal magnificence that inhabits heaven.

THIS MORNING I FEEL GOOD

Blessed are those who mourn, for they will be comforted.

MATTHEW 5:4

Sometimes, it seems, we "believe" a verse in Scripture, but when it proves true, we feel genuinely surprised.

We may have struggled in our walk with Christ and find ourselves subconsciously convinced that our lot in life consists of increasing difficulty. This feeling of perpetual sadness seems especially prevalent after the loss of a loved one. Our loss feels so great that we can't even imagine that we'll wake up one morning and actually feel good.

So on that day, we awake prepared to wrap the heavy shroud of death around us, fully expecting to place its gloomy weightiness over our tired shoulders once more.

But it's gone.

Perhaps one of those bright days already has dawned for you. You woke to find the sun shining, not only through your window but also inside your soul. The warmth of God's comfort so touched you that you smiled for the first time in ages. You looked in the mirror but saw no dark shadow of sadness lurking in the background. You got ready to greet the day with a spring in your step and a lilt in your voice.

But then, guilt descended.

I have often met with widows who want to talk. Eventually they get around to whispering, "Is it wrong to feel good?"

Just a few months after the sudden death of her husband, Ilene said to me over a cup of coffee, "I feel so guilty about feeling good, and I'm afraid to let any of my friends know. I think they will think I'm disloyal to my husband."

Inaccurate assumptions may cause people around a grieving person to act shocked when they hear that the bereaved feels good. They may think the person's grieving has concluded in an unusually short period of time.

Of course, if the first good day indicated the end of grieving, they might be correct. But as those of us who have lost a loved one know, grieving goes on for a very long time. The blessed relief of a good day comes and goes. Good days certainly become more frequent, but working through grief takes years.

When that sunny day dawns for you, push aside any feelings of guilt and walk in the light of God's comfort. Breathe deeply of the rarefied air of spiritual healing. Enjoy the moments of joy that fill your day.

You need not explain your rejuvenated spirit to anyone. If someone comments on your lightened countenance, just smile and say that you are indeed feeling good. Friends will be glad for you, even if they seem surprised at first.

You have joined the company of saints who receive blessings often difficult for the world to see or appreciate. The blessings are spiritual, the kind you can't explain even to yourself.

When the pain of loss still feels fresh, why are you able to wake up and feel good? What did you do differently the night before to bring morning sunshine into your soul?

Probably nothing. The comfort does not result from changed circumstances. It results as a blessing from God.

DOING WHAT YOU NEVER
THOUGHT YOU COULD

I can do everything through him who gives me strength.

PHILIPPIANS 4:13

Our car ranked as one of General Motors' failed attempts to convince the buying public to embrace diesel-fuel cars made in the United States. We had an Oldsmobile, a model so unpopular that we knew no one else who owned one.

My main complaint about the car involved the scarcity of gas stations equipped with diesel pumps. Jack had, for some quirky reason, liked that car, so we never discussed trading it in. After his death, I decided to buy a new car. I faced this adventure with a determination to be "wise as a serpent" and not fall prey to the wiles of notorious car salesmen.

I breezed through several new-car showrooms, looking only casually interested and dissuading any lengthy conversations with salesmen. I could also imagine them thinking that I couldn't be there to make a purchase anyway, because the man in my life wasn't with me. In those days, women typically steered clear of purchasing a car alone. I did have trouble imagining what it would be like to actually go into a dealership and talk about buying, because looking at cars revealed to me how little I knew about anything with a motor. Asking questions — even intelligent ones — about operation and efficiency would only have publicized my ignorance.

I decided to pray about what amount of money I'd take for my Oldsmobile and let that be the determining factor in choosing the car dealer from whom to buy a new car. Knowledgeable friends confirmed that when buying a new car and trading in a used one, all bargaining takes place around the value of the trade-in.

I checked the blue-book value of my Olds and rounded the number up slightly, arriving at $12,000 (in addition, several eager salesmen had told me they could give me that amount for my car). I felt reasonable and wise at the same time.

Eventually, I chose a Datsun station wagon with a silly talking feature: a woman's chirping voice making announcements such as "Door is ajar," "Lights are on," and my favorite, "Fuel level is dangerously low."

The salesman who spoke with me briefly when I first looked at the Datsun saw me coming in the second time. He swooped in and began his pitch. After taking my Olds out for a drive, he said, "Let me talk with my manager and see what we can do for you."

I waited in the showroom while the salesman and the manager conversed behind closed doors. When the salesman returned, he said with a smile that he could give me $9,000 for my car.

I reminded him that just the other day he had told me he could give me $12,000. His memory failed him and he launched into an explanation of why I should accept his stunning offer.

"If I could just have the keys back to my car, I'll be on my way," I said with my own smile when he finished talking. What transpired in the next half hour I never would have imagined.

The salesman kept asking me what he could do to put that shiny new Datsun in my driveway. I kept saying, "You can give me $12,000 for my Oldsmobile." He would disappear behind the manager's closed door with my car keys in hand. Then he would come out and offer me several hundred over his last offer. I gave the same response, and so it went.

Finally, the salesman ushered me into the manager's office and invited me to sit down. My car keys lay on his desk, and I felt tempted to grab them and run. The manager offered me $11,500 for my car, at which point I stood up and politely demanded my car keys.

"You are now insulting me," I said firmly. "If you can give me $11,500 for my car, you can give me $12,000."

The manager cheerily shook his head and agreed to give me $12,000. I parked the Datsun in my driveway that night.

I am not a confrontational person. I value politeness and kindness. But I learned early on after Jack died that some people want to take advantage of you. You can be assertive without being aggressive. You can do far more than you ever dreamed possible! You really can do everything through Christ, who gives you strength.

A FUNNY THING HAPPENED ON THE WAY TO HEALING

"For I know the plans I have for you," declares the LORD, "plans to prosper you and not to harm you, plans to give you hope and a future."

JEREMIAH 29:11

The moving van was due to arrive at our house around nine in the morning. As the hours ticked away, we made last-minute plans to stay another night in Ft. Lauderdale. Lisa, Lara, and I — along with Beth, our basset hound — were moving to Colorado. I longed to live somewhere with cooler weather, and while visiting a friend in Colorado, I had fallen in love with the place. If anyone had told me we'd be leaving our last home with Jack, the place where the girls' father was buried, the church and community that so greatly supported us, I never would have believed them.

But in June of 1983, three and a half years after Jack died, we found ourselves heading out. The moving van finally arrived at five-thirty that evening and finished loading well after dark. We headed for my parents' home to spend our last night in Florida.

Our move came as a surprise, but it wasn't an "unhappy event." A number of circumstances had led me to believe that a move would be good for all of us, and I felt a strong confirmation from the Lord that it was the right thing to do. Some friends and family thought I had lost my mind, but even their doubts did not dissuade me.

We knew only one other family in Colorado, but the girls and I felt excited about our new adventure. I had traveled to Colorado Springs three times to look at houses and schools. Lisa and Lara had not visited. They were ten and almost fourteen at the time, and I practiced what I called "benevolent dictatorship," with the emphasis on "benevolent." I had thought out my decision carefully and prayed long and hard. I promised the girls that if any one of us felt unhappy in our new home after a year, we could return to Florida.

And so on a Tuesday morning, one day later than scheduled, we piled into our Datsun and headed west. My AAA trip-tych lay next to me on the seat, and the girls had packed all kinds of diversions for the four-day drive to the home they'd never seen. Beth turned out to be a pretty good traveler, although we ate a few dinners in our motel rooms to keep her from howling out of loneliness.

When we reached the outskirts of Colorado Springs, Lisa and Lara grew more and more excited. In my attempts to undersell our destination, I had convinced them that we were moving to a town with a crossroads and a gas station. That had not been my intention, but in the early 1980s, Colorado Springs was much smaller than Ft. Lauderdale. They felt very excited and relieved to see a beautiful and large city.

Twenty years have passed since that arrival day, and all of us remained here until two years ago. Lara and her husband moved to Sacramento due to business opportunities, but they still visit often and love the city we chose so long ago. Lisa, her husband, and their four boys live just a few miles from my second husband, Steve, and me.

Our move turned out to bring health and healing to all of us, but it certainly didn't look like anything I had ever expected when thinking about our future soon after Jack died. In fact, early on I didn't see how I could ever leave our house and all the memories it held. Yet I found that God had another plan for us. He gave us a new start in another place, and our memories from our days in Ft. Lauderdale traveled with us.

Sometimes the idea of change is frightening. The loss of a loved one brings so much dramatic change that we really shouldn't make any major adjustments until some healing has taken place. But as the Lord heals, you may begin to think differently about changes and even consider plans you never entertained before.

I'M STILL AFRAID SOMETIMES

Be careful, keep calm and don't be afraid.

ISAIAH 7:4

It has been over twenty-three years since Jack died. I have been remarried for fourteen years, Lisa and Lara are grown, married, and have seven children between them. Wonderful relationships and productivity fill my life. The loss of my first husband has become a part of my life that impacts many aspects of what I feel and do, not in painful ways as much as in the rather normal ways any experience impacts the rest of life. And I believe that healing from that loss is as complete as it will ever be, this side of heaven.

But two days ago, an incident occurred that made the evidence of the continuing impact of loss quite apparent. Steve and I had been traveling in Ireland for a few weeks, combining vacationing with research for future projects. We were visiting an area in County Donegal renown for its stunning cliffs that jut out over the Atlantic Ocean with breathtaking drama. A fear of heights dampens my enthusiasm for climbing, but I try to moderate my fear and accompany Steve as far as my anxiety allows me to go.

After a particularly chilling drive on hairpin turns overlooking steep drops into the ocean far below the road, I gratefully stepped out of the car. Things looked even better than expected as we started up a gently sloping path with wide stone steps ascending the side of the mountain. The path lay inland far enough to block the drop-off from our line of vision. We stopped and sat down at a beautiful spot along the way, talked, and ate a snack. Steve scanned the path above us with binoculars.

"There are people up there," he said in an optimistic voice, pointing to a peak off in the distance.

I knew what was coming and tried to prepare myself for the next part of our excursion. As we climbed higher, the wind grew stronger. The sensation scared me, and I turned back after trying to persuade Steve to do the same. But he climbed happily up as I headed back down. The wind howled and blew across the cliffs, making sure footing difficult.

I reached a relatively calm spot, stopped, and looked back at the incline Steve had ascended. I couldn't see him, and from my perspective, the path looked dangerously near the edge of the cliff. My apprehension grew and old feelings of fear simmered, turning logical thought into anxiety.

I have been here before, I thought. *He might fall and die.*

My intellect branded my fears unreasonable. Other people had taken the same path he walked. The wind felt strong, but not strong enough to blow him off the mountain. My self-talk failed to calm me. I felt afraid, anxious, awful.

In about an hour, Steve's familiar silhouette appeared on the hilltop horizon. I breathed a sigh of relief and scolded myself for allowing fearful thoughts to overtake me. Even after so many years, some situations still cause me to relive those feelings I had the day that Jack died.

You may experience similar moments as you live with the impact of your loss. If you lost your loved one through illness, you may find that the smallest sign of poor health distresses you.

I have found that I can do little when these feelings pop up. I pray, rerun logical thoughts through my mind, try to think positively, and finally just ask God to allow the time to pass quickly until my fears subside. I do not suffer from full-blown anxiety attacks, but I would seek medical help if I did. Anxiety attacks can cause shortness of breath, rapid heart rate, and feelings of dizziness. Check with your doctor if you experience these symptoms.

More likely, you may find that feelings of fear associated with loss will occur now and then. When they do, realize that they will pass, and pray for an awareness of God's presence.

PEERING DOWN FROM HEAVEN

Therefore, since we are surrounded by such a great cloud of witnesses, let us throw off everything that hinders and the sin that so easily entangles, and let us run with perseverance the race marked out for us.

HEBREWS 12:1

I just finished reading *The Lovely Bones*, a novel by Alice Sebold that has now been on the *New York Times* best-seller list for more than fifty weeks. It tells the story of Susie, a murdered young girl who then looks down on the comings and goings of her family and friends from her spot in heaven.

While this book pays little attention to theological accuracy, it does present a picture that many of us would like to believe is at least partially true. We still want connection with our loved ones; we want them to remain part of our world somehow.

In *The Lovely Bones*, Susie's family and friends don't know when she lingers nearby except for the occasional sense of her presence. When healing for those left on earth seems to have transformed pain to bittersweet memories, Susie leaves her heavenly perch, stops watching them, and wanders in other heavenly realms. Every once in a while, she peeks back down and checks in on her loved ones, but for the most part, her life in heaven and theirs on earth remain separate.

Despite the disturbing events that end Susie's life, this story draws the reader into a warm circle of spiritual musings that narrow the gap between the living and the departed. Perhaps that is why this book has stayed on the best-seller list for such a long time.

Those of us who base our hope on our relationship with Jesus and rely on the Word of God to inform us can look at Hebrews 12:1 and do our own musing about whether loved ones in heaven see us as we live here on earth. We shouldn't attempt to contact the dead or dabble in questionable spirituality that strays from biblical teaching, of course, but I'm quite sure that we remain ignorant of some important spiritual realities. Hebrews 11 and 12 mention a gallery of God's faithful, and their faithfulness encourages us to persevere in our own race on earth. No one can say for sure whether Hebrews 12:1 implies that our loved ones watch us from above.

At the same time, I know many people, including myself, who from time to time have found comfort in a sense of their departed loved one's presence. That presence may be no more than awakened memories stirring as a result of a particularly poignant event. When my second grandchild, Alex, was born on Jack's birthday, I felt very close to Jack. I didn't see a vision or hear a voice, but it simply felt as though he were present.

That sense of presence may also be the Holy Spirit touching our souls in a deep way as we connect something happening here with the memory of our loved one. Many of the mysteries of God lie beyond our knowledge or understanding.

It is important not to live in a fantasy world or be tempted to employ the dark tactics of channelers or attend a séance. At the same time, we can feel comforted by the words of Hebrews 12:1 and praise God for the "cloud of witnesses" who went before us.

PEACE AND PAIN ARE PARTNERS

We are hard pressed on every side, but not crushed; perplexed, but not in despair.
2 CORINTHIANS 4:8

The sunshine sparkled down on San Diego, California, on December 17, 1993, and reflected off the water surrounding this beautiful city. We had been in town for almost a week in preparation for Lara's wedding, and now the big day had arrived.

Friends from across the country had flown in, and many of Craig and Lara's college friends had come. Happiness and merriment filled the air, and God's goodness poured out on these two young people as they started their lives together.

Lara and her attendants busily dressed and primped in one of the rooms of the church. I hustled around trying to help in any way I could. Curling irons got plugged in to every available outlet, and the fragrance of mingled perfumes scented every corner. High heels and velvet dresses replaced shorts and sneakers.

The photographer knocked lightly on the door and asked for everyone to come out into the church garden for pictures. Lara looked gorgeous as she walked outside, her sister and girlfriends holding up the hem of her dress. Her bouquet cascaded roses and lilies as the perfect accent to her wedding ensemble.

I returned to the room to retrieve my own camera, and when I walked out the door again, I stopped abruptly. Lara had posed for the photographer, bouquet in front of her, head tilted, when she suddenly broke her pose and uttered a small gasp. She opened her arms and tears streamed down her face. I felt the heat rush to my cheeks as I wondered what had gone wrong and prayed that she wouldn't weep makeup onto her dress.

Just as I started toward her, her Uncle Bud came into view. Jack had carried an amazing resemblance to his older brother, and now that resemblance shone out every time we looked at Bud. We saw traces of Jack in Bud's eyes, his smile — even in the definition of his arms.

Uncle Bud walked into Lara's embrace without saying a word. He, too, had tears mingled with a big smile. The two hugged each other for a tender, silent moment, and then he pulled back, wiped tears from each of Lara's eyes, and ambled into the church.

No one said a word. Tears fell, and the absence of a father and brother filled the silence with a bittersweet memory of what had been and who was missing on that eventful day. Soon Lara regained her composure and resumed the photo session.

I wiped my own tears and thanked God for the presence of His peace in the memory of pain. We had shared an interlude in which our loved one was acknowledged, grieved, and celebrated all at once.

So often we think that pain must be absent in order for peace to be present. We go through all kinds of mental gymnastics to deny that traces of pain linger for a lifetime instead of accepting that peace and pain work as partners. They coexist.

On Lara's wedding day, the memory of Jack brought beauty. It did not dampen anyone's spirits or spoil Lara's happiness. Her moment with her Uncle Bud expressed the emotion that so many of us felt but couldn't put into words.

The peace of God enveloped us all. It did not demand the absence of pain but rather rejoiced at the presence of the Lord in the midst of a deep pain that thereafter often appeared as a blessed memory.

GOD'S WORD BREATHES LIFE

For the word of God is living and active. Sharper than any double-edged sword, it penetrates even to dividing soul and spirit, joints and marrow.

HEBREWS 4:12

Many of us grew in the early years of our faith by memorizing Scripture. We carried printed cards on key rings so we could work on memory verses as we sat at stoplights. We took classes that included Scripture memory as part of the lesson, and we taught our children verses by putting them to music.

The power of the Word of God is difficult to explain to someone who has not hidden the Word in his heart. Memorized verses bring to mind the teachings of Scripture when we need them the most. Because we have internalized the words, we don't even need to struggle to recall the verses.

Scripture provides one of the greatest sources of comfort when you lose a loved one. When you find yourself in a situation in which you can't read, the verses tucked in the creases of your heart come to mind automatically and draw you close to the One who comforts most.

On index cards, I used to write verses that touched me deeply and then I'd carry them with me. That occurred in the days before home computers, but I would do the same thing again today. Something about handwriting helps you assimilate material in ways that technology simply can't provide. The very fact that it takes longer to write out a verse than it does to type it may help you retain it. You also experience the sensation of touch and express yourself creatively with your handwriting.

The Word of God copied from the Bible becomes more personally yours. You likely choose verses that mean something particular to you, resonate with you, and bring you closer to God.

I used to carry my index cards in a small metal box the same size as the cards. It's very old-fashioned now, but I look at it with fondness. The cards inside look slightly yellowed.

Now the box sits next to me on my desk. The verses on the first two cards are two of my favorites:

> I will lie down and sleep in peace,
>   for you alone, O LORD,
>   make me dwell in safety. (Psalm 4:8)

> Some trust in chariots and some in horses,
>   but we trust in the name of the LORD our God.
>   (Psalm 20:7)

The stack of cards measures about four inches thick. I accumulated them for weeks after Jack died and carried them with me for years. Just recently, I loaned about one inch's worth to a deeply hurting friend, and she made her own set of cards.

It really doesn't matter what method you use to access God's Word. The important thing is to have it at hand when you need it. Whether you memorize Scripture or keep verses with you that touch your spirit, draw on their comfort often. The power behind them will make a big part of your healing possible and will give you direction as you move through this painful time and into the future that God has in store for you.

COMFORTING OTHERS

Praise be to the God and Father of our Lord Jesus Christ, the Father of compassion and the God of all comfort, who comforts us in all our troubles, so that we can comfort those in any trouble with the comfort we ourselves have received from God.

2 CORINTHIANS 1:3-4

I had known Janice before her husband died, but we were not close acquaintances. I received a call several months after Janice's husband died from a good friend of hers asking if I would meet with Janice.

We did meet and talked for several hours. Janice had many questions and things she wanted to express to someone who had walked the same path.

I felt surprised and delighted a few years later when Janice remarried a wonderful man in our church, a widower himself. The two of them share a blessed union and work together in ministry. Janice continues to meet with a group of widows even though she is now married. Her role as an encourager often lifts the spirits of the others.

"I am their hope," she said to me one day when I asked her about the group.

Not all widows want to remarry, but many do. Statistically speaking, the likelihood of remarriage diminishes as we age. And far more single women participate inside the church community than do single men. But we are not limited to statistics. God is well able to overcome statistical data and bring two people together in the most unexpected ways.

Whether Janice had remarried or not, however, she had gone through a healing process and decided to reach out to others with the comfort she had received from the Lord. Being busy with children still at home doesn't prevent her from taking time to be with others on a similar path.

Words of encouragement are among the best tonics you can offer those in pain. They want to see that someone touched by tragedy can survive and even thrive.

When loss first hits, you don't have the energy or spiritual resources to reach out. You live in a season of receiving. Then, as your healing progresses and you experience God's comfort, you find that you want to help others. You want to give again, to testify to the goodness of God and to give back what you have received yourself.

Don't be afraid to move from receiving to giving. You may need to take the initiative instead of waiting to be asked to give. Needs abound. Just look around and choose some small way to reach out to those around you who could use a kind word or listening ear. God will bless you for your effort.

TOUCHES FROM SO MANY PLACES

But Jesus called the children to him and said, "Let the little children come to me, and do not hinder them, for the kingdom of God belongs to such as these."

LUKE 18:16

The call-waiting signal on my phone kept beeping. I had intended to ignore it but finally excused myself from the current conversation and clicked over.

I heard my daughter Lisa sobbing on the other end of the phone as she choked out the words, "We're on the way to the hospital. Dylan has pneumonia, the flu, strep, and a double ear infection."

"I'm on my way," I said, asking for no more details but knowing she had her hands full. She had Alex and Brady with her, and she needed support to deal with Dylan's illnesses.

Her husband, Chadd, met me in the waiting room with Alex and Brady as I entered the hospital. I relieved him so he could join Lisa and Dylan.

As things calmed down, Chadd took the two boys to stay with friends before he returned to work, and I joined Lisa and my very sick grandson. An intravenous tube hung over Dylan as a nurse strapped his little arm to a board. Dark circles framed his baby-blue eyes, and his pale skin looked almost translucent.

Thankfully, Dylan recovered from his multiple illnesses, but great stress punctuated those hospital days. Lisa and I took turns staying with him and holding him. We witnessed the inside of the pediatric ward and felt blessed by so many caring people.

Pneumonia and the flu had spread across our city, with the number of cases reaching almost epidemic proportions. It felt sad and sobering to see little people so very sick.

The words of a favorite verse came to my mind as I sat and rocked Dylan: "The kingdom of God belongs to such as these" (Luke 18:16). These: innocent, helpless, guileless, reliant on the goodness of God and His people. And goodness surrounded us.

Nurses and aides came in often to see what they could get for me as I sat, my arms propped up with pillows, holding Dylan. They would bring drinks or adjust the television or just smile and say a few words.

Then, one morning, we enjoyed an especially touching surprise visit. I heard the click of tiny toenails before I saw our visitor. A beautiful miniature collie, adorned with a tailor-made blanket over her back that read, "Pediatric Pet," came quietly into the room. Her trainer held her leash loosely as the dog stood silently, waiting to be invited over. I motioned to her and, tail wagging, she walked over close to Dylan and me. My grandson smiled a limp smile and moved his arm in her direction. That was all he could manage, but the smile on his face showed his moment of pleasure.

The trainer told me that the organization trains the dogs and then brings them into the hospital once or twice a week to cheer up the patients. A small thing, but so very touching.

I know that a special gift of mercy fills the many people who work and minister to the sick and elderly. They shed light and comfort with their very presence.

If you lost your loved one to the ravages of an illness, you must have many stories of your own about those who touched your life during that most difficult time. It is good to remember those people and thank God for their care.

TAKING A LONG VIEW

Though the fig tree does not bud
and there are no grapes on the vines,
though the olive crop fails
and the fields produce no food,
though there are no sheep in the pen
and no cattle in the stalls,
yet I will rejoice in the LORD,
I will be joyful in God my Savior.

HABAKKUK 3:17-18

Habakkuk, an ancient Hebrew prophet, learned to move from doubt to faith. He lived in Judah during the reign of Jehoiakim, an evil king, and the prophet pressed God to explain the presence of evil in the world. Habakkuk didn't understand why God allowed such evil to continue.

You may not have lost a loved one to an evil act, but we all live in a world acquainted with evil. Questions you might have about your loss could rise toward God side by side with questions from those who have suffered because of evil. The issue remains the same: God's people seeking to understand why God sometimes seems removed from the pain that touches their lives.

God answered Habakkuk like this: "For the revelation awaits an appointed time; it speaks of the end and will not prove false. Though it linger, wait for it; it will certainly come and will not delay" (Habakkuk 2:3).

It may appear to us that God's revelation as to the presence of evil in the world seems, indeed, delayed. But our view of time does not match God's view of time. That's part of the challenge for us as Christians living in the present. We are called to take one step at a time — to live in the present, not to borrow from tomorrow.

God insists that His justice will prevail over all the earth at some time in the future. Tension exists as we live in a world where evil often seems the victor.

We feel uncomfortable with this tension — and rightly so. Our world simmers like a pressure cooker, with fast-paced living and deteriorating values. The tension between godly virtue and the reality of a fraying culture should make us feel uncomfortable.

Certainly the events of 9/11 transformed the illusion of a secure nation into a truer picture, reflecting the need for homeland and international security. The dark tendrils of evil touch us all, not only by our personal loss but also by our nation's newly tenuous position in the world.

We are much like Habakkuk. We see evil and cry out to God. Our human limitations prevent us from fully understanding the ways of God, but God gives Habakkuk an answer that we can claim and cling to: Wait, and God will prevail.

Our trust in God tempers the tension produced by conscious waiting. We live in the moment, but we look beyond this world —

all that is happening around us, the death and disease and war --
and we see light at the end of the tunnel.

We know that this life is not all there is and that death has been
defeated by the Cross. Faith replaces our doubt and shows itself in
patient waiting for the things of God to be revealed. Like
Habakkuk, we can proclaim that no matter what happens, "We will
rejoice in the Lord!"

THE TEARS OF JESUS

Jesus wept.

JOHN 11:35

When we sit with a friend who understands, we receive one of the greatest comforts possible during a time of loss. We can pour out our hearts or sit silently, and we know that this person almost feels what we feel.

I can now look back with a smile at one moment that showed this kind of kindred friendship. Of course, none of us were smiling on the day Jack died, but you'll see the humor in it from the perspective of years gone by.

I had called my dear friend Susan from the scene of the accident and asked her to meet me at our house. Her shocked sobs rang through the phone lines as she told me she would arrive before we got home. As we reached our street, I recognized Susan's car at the house of a neighbor who lived a few houses away. Susan had stopped to tell the neighbor about Jack's accident.

We pulled over so I could see Susan before greeting the crowd that had gathered at our house. I walked in and Susan ran to me and hugged me tightly with both arms. I buried my face in her shoulder, and as she placed one hand on the back of my head to console me, she pushed hard. I couldn't breathe. Susan was crying and rocking both of us back and forth, and I had a momentary thought that I might join Jack sooner than expected.

It is good to enjoy a little humor when life deals such a striking blow, but Susan had intended only to convey her deep sorrow at our loss. She knew me well and wept with me. Her feelings comforted me then and still do all these years later.

We read in John 11:35, the shortest verse in the Bible, that Jesus wept. Jesus loved Lazarus and his two sisters, Mary and Martha. Lazarus's illness worsened, and by the time that Jesus arrived, he had died. Family and friends wept bitterly at the loss of Lazarus. And sitting with them and fully entering into their grief, Jesus cried His own tears of sorrow.

We know, of course, that the story didn't end there. Jesus called to Lazarus and, miraculously, Lazarus came out of the tomb. His resurrection from death testifies to the death-defeating power of Jesus.

While the scene of a resuscitated Lazarus emerging from the tomb often becomes the focus of this story, it is also important and comforting to pause at the picture of Jesus weeping with the family and friends of Lazarus.

We aren't told what Jesus said or anything else that He did. I think it is fair to assume, though, that Jesus knew He would call Lazarus back to life. But instead of immediately doing so, He stopped and joined in the emotion of the moment with the others present.

How amazing that God Himself, in the person of Christ, felt what we feel! He was right there at the scene of the loss and experienced the overwhelming grief that death produces. He wept — and then He raised His dear friend to life.

He will one day raise each of us who trust in Him — and then there will be no more need for weeping.

OUR FEELINGS ARE NOT A MEASURE OF THE TRUTH

When you pass through the waters,
I will be with you;
and when you pass through the rivers,
they will not sweep over you.
When you walk through the fire,
you will not be burned;
the flames will not set you ablaze.

ISAIAH 43:2

I was sitting in an aisle seat on a plane headed for Sacramento, my head down as I read my current travel-read. A quick flash of light shone in the cabin, coinciding with the sound of a loud thud, as if the plane had hit some small, dense object.

Everyone around me looked up and then at each other. I looked over at the people in my row, and the woman by the window said, "It was lightening. I saw it hit."

Lightening, I thought, as my mind raced back over decades to another lightening strike that caused a DuPont company plane to crash, killing a whole department. I was working as a travel agent back then, and we handled that account. It was a tragedy of massive proportions and resulted in a rule that company leadership never travel together on the same plane.

No one on my plane heading to Sacramento seemed to panic, and few spoke. We just waited and felt the fear level rise as no word came from the cockpit. A strange calm pervaded the cabin, and an eerie feeling of impending danger hung in the air.

"Well, ladies and gentlemen," a somewhat shaky voice finally announced over the speaker system, "we just took a lightening strike. It was right here by the cockpit, so we were a little startled. But we are fine. The runway is in sight."

The captain's words, meant to reassure, revealed doubt. The reference to the runway implied that we needed to land in a hurry. A strange, woody kind of smell became noticeable, and we once again looked around at each other with the silent question showing on each face: *Is that the smell of something burning?*

I had not heard of an airplane surviving a lightening strike, but the ride seemed unusually steady. I felt afraid but not panicky, which almost made me think that I had reached the end of this life. A jumble of conflicting emotions roiled within me. I didn't know what was true or what to expect.

Within minutes, we landed and everyone breathed a sigh of relief. The captain came back on sounding pretty relieved himself. He explained that the smell came from some kind of automatic fire retardant that releases whenever lightening strikes or any chance of fire exists at all.

While our plane had been hit, it had sustained no damage that jeopardized our safety in any way. And yet most of us on that flight felt less than safe after the strike.

The loss of a loved one propels us onto a roller-coaster ride with our emotions rising and falling like the cars on the tracks, or those seats that swing precariously under the thrill-ride's rails. We may feel overwhelmed with fears and doubts and wonder if we'll ever feel steady again.

After a little while, you will become accustomed to your fluc-tuating emotions and be able to trust that they will settle down. The roller-coaster ride will end, and the truth of Scripture will melt over your troubled emotions and bring you God's peace.

HIS BURDEN IS LIGHT

Come to me, all you who are weary and burdened, and I will give you rest. Take my yoke upon you and learn from me, for I am gentle and humble in heart, and you will find rest for your souls. For my yoke is easy and my burden is light.

MATTHEW 11:28-30

It's another morning, and you've come to the place where you meet with Jesus. This book accompanies your Bible and journal and your broken heart. Perhaps it's been some months since your loved one left.

Your burden now, regardless of the amount of time that has passed since your loss, is to carry the pain you never anticipated along the remaining road of your life. Others have told you that the weight will lighten, and you've felt a few of those moments when the sun has warmed your spirit and your burden has seemed a little less overwhelming. But most of the time, you know the weight remains, in one measure or another.

And so you come to meet with Jesus, to receive help along the arduous way. The promises of Scripture infuse your soul with renewed hope. You are not alone; you will experience healing; you will be reunited with your loved one. Sometimes, even very familiar verses spring to life with new meaning.

This verse in Matthew does that for me. Before my loss, I thought of weariness almost exclusively as physical weariness, the fatigue that settles in the muscles and draws the eyelids down. Then rest, usually the result of a good night's sleep, restored me. My own yoke resembled that of most of those around me — care of family, kindness to others, financial needs, health issues — all wrapped inside the doctrine of "doing-the-will-of-the-Father."

When I'd think about the burden Jesus carried, it seemed pretty heavy to me. I could not then, nor can I now, fully comprehend what it meant to die for the sins of the world. And so when considering this verse, I quickly passed over the part about the easy yoke and the light burden.

Then loss transformed weariness from physical fatigue to soul exhaustion. Escape from this exhaustion eluded me. I remember going away with a girlfriend for a weekend in the Florida Keys a few months after Jack died. I expected relief from the weariness of learning to live without him, but little changed.

My girlfriend was a great traveling companion, but no amount of relaxation, sleep, or exciting scenery even touched the weariness of my soul. The yoke of loss bore down hard on me, and the burden of living without Jack weighed heavily.

The words of this verse, "My yoke is easy and my burden is light," enticed me to look more closely at their possible meaning. Picturing a yoke similar to the ones I'd seen in pictures of oxen at work, I put myself on one side, with Jesus next to me on the other. I could feel pressure on my neck and shoulders, but it didn't seem overbearing. I imagined the weight distributed unequally, with

Jesus standing a little straighter than I, and thus bearing more of the weight. Still, He didn't labor. He walked with ease, smiling and inviting me to fall in step with Him. When my steps coincided with His, the weight of the yoke lessened even more.

It seemed to me that the burden of Jesus amounted to a willingness to restrain Himself within the confines of the yoke — to willingly do the will of His Father. And that burden felt light when not resisted. He trusted the Father.

How hard it is to trust when loss has pierced our lives! We feel as though we trusted, and look what happened. We can trust only when we look beyond our grief and believe that joy will return.

Our burden becomes one of daily telling Jesus that we will continue to walk with Him no matter what. We will submit to the will of the Father. When we do this, we can shift our focus from living without our loved one to living to do God's will.

WHAT WE DO MATTERS

Praise be to the God and Father of our Lord Jesus Christ! In his great mercy he has given us new birth into a living hope through the resurrection of Jesus Christ from the dead, and into an inheritance that can never perish, spoil or fade—kept in heaven for you, who through faith are shielded by God's power until the coming of the salvation that is ready to be revealed in the last time.

1 PETER 1:3-5

What a glorious promise! We inherit the salvation of our souls as the children of God. We will live forever in heaven with the Lord, and nothing can take that inheritance from us. If we believe in Christ, our future is secure.

And the amazing truth that accompanies this one is that we, too, leave an inheritance — and so did our loved one. The life we each live on this earth leaves an impression, an imprint, a mark that touches the lives of others through the centuries.

Most of us probably grew up thinking we didn't want to become like our parents. Can't you remember hearing your mother repeat a warning that you vowed you never would say to your own children? Then you became a parent and heard those words echo inside your own home. Your mother's words mattered; they left their imprint on you and probably were words of wise counsel.

Often, we think of the word *inheritance* with regard to money. But an inheritance means far more than receiving things of monetary value. Just think of all you treasured about your loved one and how you see evidence of that person all around you.

I always think of my mother when I smell the sweet, light scent of talcum powder. Fastidious about personal cleanliness, she used creams and lotions and perfumes in moderation but as part of her daily routine. And I love to remember seeing her touch a flimsy powder puff into a container of powder and dab it across her neck and shoulders. She'd pat some on the places she could reach on her back, and powder would sprinkle through the morning sunlight that filtered past her vanity table.

We no longer see many vanity tables, and we're warned not to use powder because it will damage our lungs as we breathe it in. But I love the stuff. It reminds me of the care my mother took in getting ready for her day. She was ready to meet anyone and presented a picture of feminine loveliness.

It's funny to think in those terms today as I sit in sweats and sneakers at my computer. I can go all day without seeing another soul. I don't feel that one way of dressing is right or wrong, but that one small aspect of what she did routinely reminds me of her. It's part of the inheritance she left to me.

We all leave an inheritance, whether we intend to or not. How wonderful if we could be more intentional about what impression we are making, what will be remembered, how we could influence others for their good! We all still have time to become intentional.

Because of our loss, we know the frailty of life and the value of intentional living. Part of the inheritance we received from our loved one is that very fact, that death is real and touches us all. Now we can take that truth and use it to the glory of God. We can intentionally touch others with His love and impact their lives in ways that draw them closer to Him.

TUCKING IN

During the fourth watch of the night Jesus went out to them, walking on the lake. When the disciples saw him walking on the lake, they were terrified. "It's a ghost," they said, and cried out in fear.

But Jesus immediately said to them: "Take courage! It is I. Don't be afraid."

"Lord, if it's you," Peter replied, "tell me to come to you on the water."

"Come," he said.

Then Peter got down out of the boat, walked on the water and came toward Jesus. But when he saw the wind, he was afraid and, beginning to sink, cried out, "Lord, save me!"

MATTHEW 14:25-30

"I'm going to go tuck in now," said the weary voice of my dear friend Claudette. We spoke by phone — I in Colorado and she in Florida.

Claudette's seven-year-old grandson, Brian, had lost his battle with a congenital disease, and she had just returned home from his memorial service. Over the years of Brian's illness, I'd seen Claudette grieve for her daughter and grandson and continually bring them before the Lord.

Claudette's faith kept her strong and focused, and she managed to keep moving through life with the ever-present threat that Brian would not remain on this earth very long. Then when the end came, my dear friend's resources had stretched to the limit.

I knew that when she said she was going to "tuck in," she would be home for a few days, or maybe longer, quietly resting in the presence of the Lord and leaning totally on Him. She wouldn't answer the phone or read or try to figure out what this loss meant to her and her extended family.

No. She would just "be."

Just "being" is difficult. I think we can really rest that confidently in the Lord only when we have exhausted all other resources in our attempts to deal with the pain of life. I think, too, that after a person dies of a long illness, the loved ones left here on this earth face an exhaustion that most simply can't understand.

To spend months and years knowing that a loved one faces illness and may not recover means to live under constant pressure. You watch your loved one suffer, and you suffer yourself. You focus on your loved one and your energy drains away.

We see in this passage of Scripture that when Peter left the boat and walked on the lake, he maintained his focus on Jesus. Not until he noticed the wind did he begin to sink. His fear pulled him down.

When a loved one languishes for a long time, your focus naturally remains on him or her. You look to Jesus often, but fear of loss and love of another draw you back to the situation in which you find yourself.

When you lose a loved one after a long illness, you relax your intensity. You can again turn and look at the Lord, with eyes only on Him. The wind subsides in your soul if you take the time to rest fully in Him for at least a short time.

"Tuck in" so well describes the posture of one resting in total repose in the arms of Jesus. Like a little child curled up in his mother's lap, the weary one leans in and closes the rest of the world out.

Tucking in is not isolation. It is not motivated out of fear or despair. Rather, it is the natural letting down of all defenses so that God alone can restore you. You still eat and move around and sit in the sun. But you remain quiet. You rest your mind as well as your body. In that kind of relaxation, your soul rests also.

At that point, the Holy Spirit has full reign to come in and gently bring healing to the places that have carried pain for so long. He ministers to your spirit and plants the seeds of love that will grow into new energy as the healing continues.

THE NEARNESS OF HEAVEN

"No eye has seen, no ear has heard, no mind has conceived what God has prepared for those who love him"—but God has revealed it to us by his Spirit.

1 CORINTHIANS 2:9-10

Those of us who have lost a loved one touch the outskirts of heaven. It is no longer a place somewhere up in the sky that occupies no part of our conscious thought; it becomes a reality that lives in our hearts and captures our imagination.

An often-repeated phrase goes something like, "You're so heavenly minded you're no earthly good." But *I* think that we are more often so earthly minded that we miss the enormous comfort and excitement within our reach when we contemplate heaven.

I admit that I find it difficult to picture heaven outside the cinematographic images that portray former mortals moving among puffy white clouds or walking on streets reminiscent of the sparkling road to Oz that Dorothy traveled as she approached the wizard.

I try to focus my thoughts of heaven more on what it might feel like to be in the presence of the Lord in a way that we can't comprehend on this earth. And the people! Just think of all the people who will be there. I am better able to imagine what it will be like to be with them, but that familiarity doesn't lessen my anticipation of what it will be like to be with God Himself.

In church, I sometimes begin to experience the revelation of heaven mentioned by the writer of 1 Corinthians 2:9-10. Being in the company of others who believe as I do reinforces the perfect corporate oneness that we will enjoy in heaven. A foretaste of that union as we gather on Sunday mornings to worship together thrills me.

We sometimes visit a church built on the model of a European cathedral. The sanctuary walls, made of gray stones, rise high above us to the base of a vaulted ceiling. Stained-glass windows adorn the walls, and a large stained-glass window stands majestically behind the altar. The brilliant colors change slightly as the sun and clouds play outside this peaceful yet awe-inspiring building.

One Sunday, the pastor drew our attention to the large stained-glass window behind the altar and talked about picturing a banquet table reaching into the sanctuary and then out past the window, stretching all the way to heaven. He talked of the banquet that we will all enjoy when we sit with the Lamb and worship Him with all the throngs who have followed Him across the ages.

Tears rolled down my face as the gap between heaven and earth closed around this image. The thought of that window opening and those of us here on earth being united with those who have gone ahead of us brought an indescribable joy to my heart. I pictured Jesus seated at the head of the table, smiling at His beloved -- all of us who believe in Him.

We live in the earthly world, and most of the time, heaven seems far away in the future. And in truth, it wouldn't be healthy to constantly sit and daydream about heaven, fulfilling the phrase about being too heavenly minded.

But on Sunday morning in the company of the saints of the Lord, it is a comfort and an inspiration to ponder the reality of heaven. It lifts our spirits and gives us hope in the future that lies ahead of us and in the present where we can glimpse the wonders of God's glory in its fullest.

TIME TO PUT THE PICTURES AWAY

Not that I have already obtained all this, or have already been made perfect, but I press on to take hold of that for which Christ Jesus took hold of me.

PHILIPPIANS 3:12

Our home had become a shrine. After Jack died, photos of him covered every available tabletop. Enlarged photos adorned every wall.

In those early days, the reminders of so much of our lives together gave the girls and me great comfort. The girls loved to look at the pictures of Jack and me from our high-school days when he was a big basketball star and I was a cheerleader. Then we had a wall section of Jack in his army gear, striding across the tarmac in his helicopter flight jacket. Chronicles of vacations and special events filled the house, making every room a bit of a pictorial museum.

After about two years, I looked around and realized that we were moving on. I understood that we didn't need the pictures anymore to try to keep Jack with us in some small way. He lived in heaven, enjoying an active existence, and I felt certain that he, too, wanted us to move on with our lives.

One day when I was listening to the radio, an old song came on with a line about looking at a photograph. I picked up the small framed photo of Jack that sat on my desk and took the photo out of the frame. I turned it over and over and swept my fingers across the image of his face again and again.

The photo paper crumpled in my hands when I squeezed it. It wasn't Jack. I cried and held the photo close to my heart and then put it in a drawer. I replaced the photo with one of Lisa and Lara playing at the beach on some recent outing. While sadness filled the moment, healing also took place. The time had arrived to turn the house into a reflection of who we were at that moment, not who we had been when Jack was with us.

On bookcases in the girls' rooms, I kept a few small photos of them together with Jack; I left one family photo in the living room. An artist had sketched a particularly lifelike picture of Jack that I hung on the wall in the hallway. These were fun and respectful reminders of Jack, but the whole house didn't need to be draped in his image.

The timing of making changes like this one depends on the individual. Perhaps you are in the early stages of grief and still need those comforting reminders of your loved one. But if years have passed, consider taking them down and redecorating. Think about making your home a warm and inviting haven for family and friends that reflects the goodness of God in the present.

I loved framing pictures of Lisa and Lara laughing during some ordinary day and others of special events in which they had taken part. As the years went by, the pictures recorded graduations and weddings. Now my house brims with pictures of our seven grand-children. I change the photos often. Photos of trips to the zoo or our oldest grandson receiving his first wrestling trophy replace the baby pictures. The only permanent portraits still on display are of Lisa and Lara in their wedding gowns.

And in each of their homes — in an inconspicuous, but frequently passed place — the girls display a copy of the artist's sketch of Jack. We all pass those pictures without comment and don't choke up at their presence. I often smile and wink when I go by on the heels of a chattering grandchild. Jack lives on in heaven, and traces of him live on in the boundless action of seven little people who now fill my heart with unlimited joy.

Your loved one lives on, too. Don't be afraid to release him or her from the walls of your home. Put up photos of your life today. This isn't betrayal. It is acknowledging the wonder of God's touch in the lives of those of us who remain.

UNANSWERED QUESTIONS

If you then, though you are evil, know how to give good gifts to your children, how
much more will your Father in heaven give the Holy Spirit to those who ask him!

LUKE 11:13

My friend Susan knew nothing about her birth father except the most basic facts revealed by her mother. Her parents had divorced when Susan was a little girl. Her mother revealed more by what she didn't say than by what she did say.

Unanswered questions haunted Susan over the years: *Why had her father left the family? What had he thought about his only daughter? Why had she and her brother never had a relationship with him after the divorce?* Some answers to her questions began to surface when Susan reached her fifties.

Her father's sister, Jean, and Susan began communicating after finding one another through Susan's stepfather. Jean and Susan talked for hours on the phone, e-mailed each other, and finally met when Susan flew to Florida. The information quenched her thirst for details like water to a thirsty traveler.

One day, a package arrived from Jean. Inside were several photos of Susan's father as well as a newspaper clipping about him leaving for World War II. The picture above the article showed her mother standing in the doorway of their home, her brother at her father's feet, and Susan wrapped lovingly in her father's arms. Her long legs gripped the tall soldier, and her arms encircled his neck. He hugged her tightly to him. The image clearly showed a father saying good-bye to a child he dearly loved.

Susan's father died years ago, so she doesn't have any firsthand information from him — but this picture speaks volumes. She never had believed that her father had had any feelings for her at all, and that particular loss had cut deeply into her soul and wounded her self-esteem. Now, as she looks at the framed picture of the little girl in the arms of her father, she knows how wrong that assumption had been.

Maybe you lost a loved one from whom you were estranged or who died years ago and left many unanswered questions. You may not find a long-lost relative to fill in the gaps or give you pictures of you with your loved one, but I hope that Susan's story gives you hope if doubts fill your mind about relationships with loved ones now gone.

You may look back and wish you had done things differently, or you may wonder how that person felt about any number of issues between the two of you. You may not find out this side of heaven what they felt, but you can trust that negative answers you tell yourself are not necessarily true. There may have been much love toward you that you didn't see or couldn't comprehend.

Luke 11:13 also speaks to the love between a parent and a child and suggests how much greater is the love of God for us. No matter whom you have lost or how damaged that relationship might have been, you now have a relationship with the God of the universe, who loves you unconditionally.

THE ABUNDANT LIFE

I have come that they may have life, and have it to the full.

JOHN 10:10

Jesus doesn't qualify His words in John 10:10. He doesn't say that you can have life "to the full" *unless* you have lost a loved one.

But how can life ever feel full again when the pain of loss pierces your very soul? The answer to that question is complex and differs for each of us. It takes a vulnerable relationship with Jesus, faith in His goodness, trust that He can and will heal you, time to move through that healing process, and a willingness to embrace the tension that exists this side of heaven.

That tension means accepting that life will not always unfold as we desire. We live in a fallen world that subjects us to the results of sin — our own and the sins of others — all the way back to Adam. We may consider this unfair as we view life from our limited perspectives, but that is how it is. And into the midst of this unfair world, God sent His Son to redeem us and give us life to the full.

As you recover from the loss you have suffered, be open to finding wholeness again. Don't insist on seeing yourself as a victim. Don't linger on how you think life should be instead of asking how to live well, given how life really is.

Look for God's abundant grace and thank Him for it. Relationship with Jesus nurtures abundant life. It has little to do with circumstances and everything to do with communing with your Lord. Take everything to Him and faithfully follow Him, no matter what difficulties come your way. Abundance of joy in your spirit will result.

Joy isn't something you feel every minute of every day, but it is a liberating reality that will permeate your life. When the lows come, you will be able to regain your perspective more quickly if you have nurtured your relationship with the Lord. Instead of seeing only the pain, you will recognize that you are in the middle of a process and that joy will return.

There is a well-known cliché that asks, "Do you see a glass half empty or half full?" The glass of water is actually both. You need not deny the pain of life to experience abundance, but you do need to realize the fullness that is also present. And to experience any of that fullness, you need to drink from that fullness. The goodness of God is available, but He does not force-feed you.

Nurture your relationship with Him and allow Him to bring His abundance into even the most painful circumstances.

A NEW HEAVEN AND
A NEW EARTH

Then I saw a new heaven and a new earth, for the first heaven and the first earth
had passed away, and there was no longer any sea. I saw the Holy City, the new
Jerusalem, coming down out of heaven from God, prepared as a bride beautifully
dressed for her husband. And I heard a loud voice from the throne saying, "Now
the dwelling of God is with men, and he will live with them. They will be his
people, and God himself will be with them and be their God. He will wipe every
tear from their eyes. There will be no more death or mourning or crying or pain,
for the old order of things has passed away."

He who was seated on the throne said, "I am making everything new!"

REVELATION 21:1-5

Revelation 21:1-5 is one of my very favorite Scripture passages. The
scene it paints promises us life without the tension between peace
and pain. God will live with us, never far off. No more death, no
more pain. Everything will be new.

When we visited the Holy Land, our tour bus drove into
Jerusalem one evening just as dusk fell. Our driver put on a tape as
the Holy City came into view, and the strains of the song "Jerusalem"
played in the background as we first looked upon the famous and
sacred place so often a part of Scripture's story of God on earth.

Twinkling lights grew in number as darkness turned dusk to night and the residents of Jerusalem lit their homes. The music in the background enhanced a sense of the historic importance of the place we were approaching, and many of us took out tissue to wipe the tears from our eyes. This deeply moving sight stirred us all, and a hushed silence fell on our group.

Yet that sight pales in comparison to what we will see when the Lord returns and establishes the new Jerusalem. We, His chosen children, will live forever in His light. The darkness will vanish, and the majesty of God will light the new heaven and the new earth.

I think back to how I felt as I first glimpsed the site of Jesus' last days on this earth, and I'm astounded that we're a privileged part of His story. It excites me to contemplate that the site of His death was also the site of His resurrection, and because of that fact, we will live forever.

As you walk through the days and live through the nights of loss, keep the image of a new heaven and a new earth near in your mind. Your pain will one day completely fade. You will be reunited with your loved one in the presence of the Lord. The time of pain here will seem but the wink of an eye compared to the eternal future that lies ahead.

God is making everything new!

EPILOGUE

I tell you the truth, you will weep and mourn while the world rejoices. You will grieve, but your grief will turn to joy. A woman giving birth to a child has pain because her time has come; but when her baby is born she forgets the anguish because of her joy that a child is born into the world. So with you: Now is your time of grief, but I will see you again and you will rejoice, and no one will take away your joy.

JOHN 16:20-22

No matter where you are in the grieving process, you will come to a place where life is good again. You will have integrated the truth of Scripture with the reality of your loss and emerged with fresh hope.

The worries of life that all of us face will touch you and bring new challenges. But you have walked through the deepest of valleys and come through whole. The breath of heaven that sweeps over you from time to time will remind you that you can overcome each new challenge with God's help.

Rejoice in that! Live full, live well, and stay close to Jesus.

About the Author

Lois Rabey has been writing and speaking for more than twenty years on a wide range of topics. Her ministry began when her first husband was tragically killed in a hot-air-balloon accident, leaving Lois to raise their two young daughters.

Moments for Those Who Have Lost a Loved One, Lois's ninth book, brings hope and comfort to those who have suffered similar losses. Lois brings to the reader her own experience as well as the experiences of others who know the grief of loss.

Lois is married to writer Steve Rabey and has two married daughters and seven grandchildren. The Rabeys live in Colorado Springs, Colorado.

From New Life Ministries
founder Steve Arterburn,

"If you're in trouble, anytime, we're here to help..."

Someone who cares
is always there at
1-800-NEW-LIFE

Other books in the
NEW LIFE LIVE! MEDITATIONS series.

Moments for Couples Who Long for Children

With encouraging stories and helpful advice, Ginger Garrett, who has battled infertility herself, gently leads couples to a new sense of hope in God's compassion.
by Ginger Garrett   1-57683-472-7

Moments for Families with Prodigals

How can you help your son or daughter who has wandered from God? This book helps you claim scriptural promises and shows how you can participate in God's work in your prodigal's life.
by Robert J. Morgan   1-57683-473-5

Moments for Singles

Sincere and heartfelt, these insightful devotions challenge singles to live vulnerable, purposeful lives before God.
by Leigh McLeroy   1-57683-540-5

To order copies, visit your local Christian bookstore,
call NavPress at 1-800-366-7788, or log on to www.navpress.com.

To locate a Christian bookstore near you,
call 1-800-991-7747.

New Life Live! Meditations

NAVPRESS ®
BRINGING TRUTH TO LIFE
www.navpress.com